WE ARE
GOD'S
UNIQUE
INTIMACY

WE ARE GOD'S UNIQUE INTIMACY

RESTORING ALLUREMENT AND INTIMACY AS CORE STRUCTURES OF COSMOS

PARTICIPATING IN THE EVOLUTION OF LOVE THROUGH UNIQUE SELF SYMPHONY

• • •

From Conscious Evolution 1.0 to Conscious Evolution 2.0

One Mountain, Many Paths: Oral Essays
Volume Six

DR. MARC GAFNI AND BARBARA MARX HUBBARD

Authors: Marc Gafni and Barbara Marx Hubbard
Title: We Are God's Unique Intimacy
From Conscious Evolution 1.0 to Conscious Evolution 2.0

Identifiers: ISBN 979-8-88834-066-0 (electronic)
ISBN 979-8-88834-065-3 (paperback)

Edited by Kristina Amelong, Timothy Paul Aryeh,
Dorothea Betz, and Christopher Nelson

World Philosophy and Religion Press,
in conjunction with

IP Integral Publishers

https://worldphilosophyandreligion.org

JOIN THE REVOLUTION!

CONTENTS

CHAPTER 6   **WE ARE GOD'S UNIQUE INTIMACY AND GOD'S POWER**

CHAPTER 7   **ALLUREMENT, INTIMACY AND EVOLUTION**

CHAPTER 8   **ALLUREMENT, AMAZEMENT AND EVER INCREASING INTIMACY**

EDITORIAL NOTE ABOUT AUTHORSHIP, EDITING, AND THE RADICAL CONTEXT FOR THIS SERIES

ORAL ESSAYS FROM THE ONE MOUNTAIN, MANY PATHS WEEKLY BROADCAST

This volume is part of the Oral Essays library, a series of lightly edited, compiled transcripts of oral teachings given by Dr. Marc Gafni and the late Barbara Marx Hubbard in their weekly online broadcast, *One Mountain, Many Paths,* which they co-founded in 2017. Originally called an "Evolutionary Church," *One Mountain, Many Paths* became a key venue for the articulation of an inspired and deeply grounded new Story of Value in response to the meta-crisis. Marc and Barbara—together with Zak Stein,[1] Kristina Kincaid, Ken Wilber, Sally Kempton, Lori Galperin, Aubrey Marcus and dozens of other thought-leaders over the years—began to articulate what they call a World Philosophy and World Religion[2] as a context for our diversity.

---

1 Zak, together with Ken Wilber, has been Marc's primary intellectual partner and an initiate lineage holder in CosmoErotic Humanism.
2 This project is grounded in four core organizational frameworks: 1) The Center for World Philosophy and Religion, co-founded by Marc Gafni, Zachary Stein, Sally Kempton, and Ken Wilber, and chaired over the years by John P. Mackey, Barbara Marx Hubbard, Aubrey Marcus, Gabrielle Anwar and Shareef Malnik, Carrie Kish and Adam Bellow, and Kathleen J. Brownback. 2) The Office for the Future, chaired by Stephanie Valcke and Ivan Bossyut. 3) The World Philosophy and Religion Press, founded and chaired by Aubrey Marcus, together with Marc Gafni and Zachary Stein. 4) The Foundation for Conscious Evolution, founded by Barbara Marx Hubbard and currently chaired by Peter Fiekowsky. For a complete list of key leadership, see the Office for the Future website, www.officeforthefuture.com.

Until Barbara's passing in 2019, she and Marc transmitted teachings together as evolutionary partners and "whole mates," weaving together insights and transmissions from their decades of practice, study, teaching, and activism into a synergy of wisdom, a grounded vision for future policy across all sectors of society.

Much of the *dharma* material below comes directly from Marc, so it was originally all in quotation marks—but that looked a little odd. So per his suggestion we removed them, and the reader should consider the paragraphs on the next several pages as one extended quote from him. We are joyfully grateful to Marc for the clarity of his Dharma, the elegance and "second simplicity" of this language, and the mad, Outrageous Love with which he transmits his teachings.

Barbara and Marc called the mission of *One Mountain* "a Planetary Awakening in Evolutionary Love Through Unique Self Symphonies." We are an evolutionary community with a deeply grounded, radically alive, and "post-tragic" revolutionary spirit. We are activating a new humanity and awakening as a new species: *Homo amor*, the fulfillment of *Homo sapiens*.

One Mountain is committed to articulating a Story of Value that can become the ground for the new society that must be birthed in response to the meta-crisis. We recognize that we are living at a pivotal moment in history. In this "time between stories," the great moral imperative is to tell the new Story of Value. It is ours to do, personally and collectively, with great trembling and ecstatic joy.

FROM DOGMA TO DHARMA: ETERNAL AND EVOLVING FIRST PRINCIPLES AND FIRST VALUES

The teachings are grounded in decades of deep study across many wisdom traditions. Over the years, week by week, these teachings were incrementally developed within the framework of the *One Mountain, Many Paths* broadcast. We often refer to these teachings as *Dharma*.

This word was originally used in lineage traditions to refer to something like universal law. This is a crucial realization: just as there is universal law in mathematical value, there is also a sense of universal law in ethics and value.

Historically, Dharma often devolved into unchanging dogma. Evolution was ignored, and the natural process of Dharma evolution became disconnected from its deep, eternal context. The weakness of the word Dharma is that too often it did not include the evolving insights of the sciences, it confused local cultural truths with universal truths, and it used words like "eternal," as in "eternal Tao," as opposed to words like "evolution."

Eternal came to mean unchanging, and that kind of thinking often led to overly ethnocentric readings of Dharma. Local systems would claim their religious and cultural insights as immutable, which stood in the way of the emergence of a genuine world Story of Value that is real, inherent to Cosmos, and backed by the Universe—even as it is also always evolving.

Or, as we often say, "eternal value is evolving value. The eternal Tao is the evolving Tao."

We have shown that, emergent from profound insights in the "interior sciences," eternal does not mean unchanging in time; it means what we call the deeper Field of ErosValue that is beneath culture, geography, and history, which lives beneath all individual and collective values, and beneath time and space itself.

As such, we have gradually transitioned from the term Dharma to the term *Value*, in the sense of the Field of Value that lives beneath all values. This Field of Value discloses as First Principles and First Values embedded in a Story of Value.

Indeed, as the interior sciences knew and the exterior sciences imply, Reality arises in a Field of ErosValue in which an entire set of mathematical, musical, molecular, moral, and mystical values are the very ground of all being. That Field of Value is eternal—the true ground of the Good, True and Beautiful—even as it is evolving.

But of course, it is equally critical not just to talk about evolving value, but to ground the evolving value in its true nature, the eternal Field of First Principles and First Values, always reaching for ever-more life, ever-more love, ever-more care, ever-more depth, ever-more uniqueness, ever-more intimate communion, and ever-more transformation.

As such, when we refer to the word Dharma, which still appears in these texts together with the word value, we refer to an evolving Dharma grounded in an *eternal and evolving* Field of Value. Indeed, eternity and evolution are two faces of the whole, opposites joined at the hip, that characterize the nature of our Cosmos in virtually all of its expressions.

It's in these terms that we ground a robust world philosophy that integrates the validated, leading-edge insights of premodern traditional wisdom, modern wisdom, and more recent postmodern insights, weaving them together into a new whole greater than the sum of its parts.

This new whole is a shared Story of Value rooted in First Principles and First Values that are both eternal and evolving.

These First Principles and First Values of Cosmos are woven together into a new Story of Value as a context for our diversity, a new Universe Story. This new Story gives us the best possible responses we have to the mystery, and to the great questions:

- Who am I? Who are we?
- Where am I? Where are we?
- What should I do? What should we do?

It is only through such a shared Universe Story—a narrative of identity and ethos as a context for our blessed diversity—that we can realize how what unites is so much greater than what divides us.

Only a new Story of Value will allow us to both respond to the meta-crisis and participate together in birthing the most true, good, and beautiful world that we already know is possible.

THIS ORAL ESSAYS SERIES IS AN ENTRYWAY TO THE GREAT LIBRARY OF COSMOEROTIC HUMANISM

This Oral Essays series is part of the overarching project of the Great Library at the Center for World Philosophy and Religion, led by Dr. Marc Gafni, together with Dr. Zak Stein. The aim of the Great Library project is to articulate a robust and comprehensive new Story of Value, CosmoErotic Humanism, in the form of dozens of well-researched and extensively footnoted academic works.

Our vision is to provide the philosophical framework that will be vital for navigating humanity through this time of immense crisis and transformation.

To begin your journey into CosmoErotic Humanism, we tenderly refer you to the book *First Principles and First Values*, co-authored by Marc Gafni, Zak Stein, and Ken Wilber, under the name David J. Temple. David J. Temple is a pseudonym created for enabling ongoing collaborative authorship at the Center for World Philosophy and Religion. The two primary authors behind David J. Temple are Marc Gafni and Zak Stein, and for different projects, specific writers will be named as part of the collaboration, such as Ken Wilber and others.

Three other volumes complete this introduction: *A Return to Eros*, by Marc Gafni and Kristina Kincaid; *Your Unique Self*, by Marc Gafni; and *Education in a Time between Worlds*, by Zak Stein.

We hope that the Oral Essays in this volume, with their informal style of transmission, will serve as an allurement and entryway for you into the more formal books of the Great Library that provide the robust intellectual underpinnings of the new Story of Value.

A NOTE ABOUT THE EDITORS

This Oral Essays collection has been edited by students of the new Story of CosmoErotic Humanism. Each of us has actively participated in *One Mountain, Many Paths*, and most of us have been in deep "Holy of Holies" study with Dr. Marc Gafni for many years.

We have been privileged to find ourselves well-versed in the teachings, and even emerging as lineage-holders of CosmoErotic Humanism.[3]

We view this editing project as a privilege and a deep practice of study and clarification. We experience ourselves as a *mystical editing society*, frequently meeting and conversing together about the content—the depth of knowledge and wisdom offered here—as well as the technical intricacies involved with publishing a beautiful and coherent series of books. In so

---

3 CosmoErotic Humanism is a world philosophical movement aimed at reconstructing the collapse of value at the core of global culture. Much like Romanticism or Existentialism, CosmoErotic Humanism is not merely a theory but a movement that changes the very mood of Reality. It is an invitation to participate in evolving the source code of consciousness and culture towards a cosmocentric *ethos* for a planetary civilization.

The term CosmoErotic Humanism, initially coined by Dr. Gafni and colleagues, points to a complex, multi-faceted, layered, and nuanced evolutionary set of insights that has evolved over decades of intensive research, teaching, and spiritual practice from deep within a wide range of wisdom traditions (including the Wisdom of Solomon lineage tradition, Bodhisattva Buddhism, and Kashmir Shaivism), as well as multiple disciplines including complexity theory, chaos theory, emergence theory, molecular biology, and the more classical disciplines of the humanities.

The seeds of CosmoErotic Humanism were planted with Dr. Marc Gafni's work on a two-volume, 1,000-page opus called *Radical Kabbalah* (Integral Publishers, 2012). This scholarly work, sourced from deep study within the esoteric lineage texts of the Wisdom of Solomon, points to a non-dual, or acosmic, realization which—unlike the prevailing conceptualization of non-duality—does not efface the human being; rather, it is highly humanistic in its nature. The next step in the evolution of CosmoErotic Humanism was the insight that all of Reality is evolving Eros, which lives in, as, and through the human being.

A failure of Eros leads inexorably to the creation of narratives of "pseudo-eros." CosmoErotic Humanism is a response to the modern mental and social breakdown sourced in the proliferation of multiple forms of pseudo-eros and its broken narratives, such as rivalrous conflict governed by win/lose metrics and the dogmatic denial of intrinsic value in Cosmos, which together generate our current "global intimacy disorder."

doing, we function as a "Unique Self Symphony," which itself is a Dharmic term that connotes an omni-considerate collaboration between realized Unique Selves synergizing our unique gifts into a new emergence greater than the sum of the parts. Even as we worked diligently to standardize our editing styles, meeting on a weekly basis to debate the nuances of phrasing, we also operated from within a deep appreciation of the unique style that each editor brought to his or her work. As such, the reader might notice some variation in editing style among the books.

Please note that Dr. Marc Gafni has not reviewed these edited Oral Essays, as he is deeply engaged in writing the formal books of the Great Library. But he has been generous in responding to questions and providing overall guidance in the project. Overall, as Marc's students and students of the Dharma, we have made it a key project at the Center to publish these pieces of work relatively independently.

OUR UNIQUE ORAL-ESSAY EDITING STYLE PRESERVES THE ENERGY OF THE ORIGINAL TRANSMISSION

Dr. Marc Gafni is a uniquely gifted teacher whose oral transmission is imbued with a quality that has proven transformative for his students. Many of us feel mystically transformed by both the content and the underlying energy of the transmission style. Therefore, as we like to say, *trust the magic ways the Dharma comes through your unique understanding!*

As Marc's empowered students, colleagues, and beloved friends, we have a deep knowing that these teachings are vital for the survival and thriving of humanity as we know it, and we recognize the importance of publishing his teachings in a written format that will be accessible by future generations. At the same time, we sought to preserve the Eros of the original oral transmission with all of its nuance, power, and depth. Our intention in the editing process, to the greatest extent possible, has been to keep these spoken artifacts intact in order to maintain the flow of the original transmission. We have therefore chosen not to engage in intensive formal editing, as we found that doing so resulted in the loss of the energetic transmission that is so key to fully receiving the Dharma.

After experimenting with many ways to present these texts, we developed a specific way of laying out the text on the page. Marc, in collaboration with Zak Stein and Russian intellectual/artist Elena Maslova-Levin—and ultimately all of the editors, through many conversations—developed a unique, artistic presentation of the text, using bolding, italics, bullet points, and other stylistic features which together serve to accentuate the immediacy of the oral transmission.

As part of this editing style, intended to preserve the integrity of the original transmission, we have refrained from removing the frequent recapitulations of key themes. We found that each recapitulation contributes something vital to the rhythm and music beneath the words, like the beating drum of our hearts. These recapitulations not only review previous material but also add important new emphases, perspectives, and elements of the new Story of Value. We ask for your patience as a reader to trust the rhythm of these texts, and we trust you as a reader to have the depth and steadiness to find your way through.

KEY COMPONENTS: LINK TO THE ORIGINAL BROADCAST, EVOLUTIONARY LOVE CODES AND PRAYER

To supplement the written word, each episode includes a QR code linking to the original broadcast on YouTube, as well as occasional links to featured songs and video clips.

Each episode also centers around an "Evolutionary Love Code," formulated by Marc. These codes are part of the ongoing articulation and distillation of the Dharma as it unfolds and emerges, week by week, over the course of many years, through the mystical process we call Outrageous Love or Evolutionary Love.

Another core component of the *One Mountain, Many Paths* episodes is what Marc and Barbara called "Evolutionary Prayer." Prayer is experienced in *One Mountain* not in the old fundamentalist sense of a "cosmic vending-machine god" who is alienated from Cosmos. Marc refers to this as the "god you do not and should not believe in"—and he often adds, "the god you don't believe in does not exist."

GOD IS THE INFINITE INTIMATE

In fact, in the Dharma of CosmoErotic Humanism, a new name for God has emerged: the "Infinite Intimate," who appears in first-, second-, and third-person expressions. Marc first shared this name as he heard it whispered in 2023, although earlier intimations and formulations of the name appeared as early as 2010.

In first person, God is infinitely alive and as intimate as our own first-person experience.

In second person, God is the infinitely intimate Personhood of Cosmos that knows our name and holds us—the God about whom we say, *whenever we fall, we fall into Her hands.* This is the God who is our Beloved, Father, Mother, Lover, and Evolutionary Partner.

Finally, in third person, God inheres in all of the First Principles and First Values of Cosmos, and in the laws of science (both interior and exterior) that govern manifest Reality.

Therefore, we have a realization of God as not only the Infinity of Power but also the Infinity of Intimacy.

In *One Mountain, Many Paths*, we are reclaiming prayer at a higher level of consciousness. And we are reclaiming prayer as deep, alive, loving, and intimate conversations with God as the Infinite Intimate who knows our name.

REFLECTING ON THE CO-CREATION BETWEEN DR. MARC GAFNI AND BARBARA MARX HUBBARD

Barbara and Marc met five years before Barbara passed. As Barbara said so often, "before I met Marc, I was sure that I was done." Barbara had taught so beautifully for decades, focusing particularly on a powerful articulation of "conscious evolution." Indeed, it would not be inaccurate to say that Barbara was the greatest storyteller of conscious evolution of her time.

Conscious evolution was also a premise in Marc's thinking, but drawn from an entirely different set of sources and experiences. Barbara drew from the classical sources of evolutionary spirituality, such as Teilhard de Chardin, Buckminster Fuller, and many others. Indeed, she was closely associated with Fuller, and was perhaps de Chardin's most ardent intellectual devotee.

Marc drew a somewhat different vision of conscious evolution from the interior sciences of the great wisdom traditions, with a primary emphasis on what he refers to as the "Solomon lineages," merged together with careful readings of the leading edges of the sciences. In the old version of conscious evolution, the movement from unconscious to conscious was a movement of evolution by chance to evolution by choice. Together Marc and Barbara evolved the old version of Conscious Evolution, pointing out that evolution itself was always in some sense conscious, but as Marc formulated it, the awakening to conscious evolution refers to the awakening of evolution as human consciousness, coupled with the human realization of being conscious evolution in person, and the human capacity to locate oneself within the context of the larger evolutionary story.

Marc focused his attention on an entirely different dimension of Reality, which he and his colleagues began to call CosmoErotic Humanism. The Intimate Universe, Homo amor, Unique Self and Unique Self Symphonies, God as the Infinity of Intimacy, Eros and the CosmoErotic Universe, distinctions like Role Mate, Soul Mate and Whole Mate, the Four Selves, Evolutionary Love, Outrageous Love, Evolution: the Love Story of the Universe, First Principles and First Values, Evolving Perennialism, the

Evolution of Love, and many more are terms articulated by Gafni and shared with Barbara in their conversation, study, and creative engagement.

Some terms they coined together, for example "a Planetary Awakening in Love through Unique Self Symphonies," where Gafni described Unique Self Symphonies, and Barbara aligned her vision of a planetary Pentecost to Marc's vision of Unique Self Symphonies.

Other key terms were unique and articulated by Barbara, for example: conscious evolution, teleros, telerotic, from joining genes to joining genius, regenopause, vocational arousal, birthing of humanity, synergy engine, and of course her work around what she called the Wheel of Co-creation. Ultimately, Marc and Barbara attempted to synergize their work in what they called the Wheel of Co-creation 2.0. Barbara and Marc experienced themselves as merging their respective Dharma into what they began to refer to as Conscious Evolution 2.0, or later, CosmoErotic Humanism.

The first 129 episodes of One Mountain, Many Paths took place in the last period of Barbara's life and reflect the depth and texture of the stunning evolutionary whole-mate meeting between her and Marc. As Barbara was deep in study with Marc, a lot of what she shared in Evolutionary Church was the Dharma of their deep study and collaboration. Although sometimes it may be clear who is speaking, we generally publish these early episodes in what we are calling "one voice." The first 129 episodes, with Marc and Barbara together, have been grouped chronologically. Episodes 130 to 400 and onwards, which were transmitted by Marc, have been grouped by topic.

THE INVITATION

We invite you to find your way into this revolution. Each one of our Unique Selves and unique gifts are desperately needed as we co-create this new Story of Value together, as part of the covenant between generations, for the sake of the whole.

Let's *play a larger game* and evolve the very source code of consciousness and culture together.

With mad love,

The Editors

LOVE OR DIE

LOCATING OURSELVES: ARTICULATING THE ESSENTIAL CONTEXT FOR THE ONE MOUNTAIN, MANY PATHS ORAL ESSAYS

SETTING OUR INTENTION

Intention setting is everything.

We're here—as da Vinci was with his cohort in the Renaissance—**to play a larger game, to participate in the evolution of love, which is to tell the new Story of Value rooted in First Principles and First Values.**

- Our intention is to recognize the critical historical juncture in which we find ourselves.
- Our intention is to take our seat at the table of history and to say, *we take responsibility for this.*
- Our intention is to participate as revolutionaries for the sake of the whole.

What we're here to do is revolution; revolution for the sake of the evolution of love.

It's a revolution for the sake of the trillions of unborn lives that will not manifest:

- The unborn loves
- The unborn creativity
- The unborn goodness
- The unborn truth
- The unborn beauty

All of it looks to us.

Not because we're engaged in grandiosity. Not at all!

- We're trembling before She.
- We're trembling with joy at the privilege.
- We're trembling with joy at the responsibility.
- We're trembling with joy at the Possibility of Possibility.
- We have to enact a new Story in this moment of time. Because it is only a new Story that can change the vector of history.

The most revolutionary act that we can do—the greatest moral imperative of this time—**is to articulate a new Story at this time between worlds and this time between stories.**

Story is not made up, as postmodernity suggests. **We all live in inescapable frameworks; our framework is the story we live in.** Right now, Reality lives according to win/lose metrics, a story that is generating existential risk. **We need to change that story.**

When we change that story, when we tell a new Story—not a made-up story, but a new Story of Value, rooted in First Principles and First Values—**then it all changes.**

We need to participate in the evolution of the source code of consciousness and culture, which is the evolution of love.

It's the most important, exciting, evolutionary, revolutionary act that we can do to alleviate suffering: to be lovers.

Like Rumi, the great poet of Sufism, we have to be "mad lovers," because it's the only sanity.

To be mad lovers is to see around the corner, to not be so obsessed with the details of the contractions of my life.

Let me see bigger.

Let me take complete care of myself in every possible way, let me completely attend to those in my circle of intimacy and influence, and then—*let me expand my circle.*

That's what we're here for.

- ◆ Our intention is to participate in the *LoveForce,* the *LoveIntelligence,* the *LoveBeauty,* the *LoveDesire* that literally animates Cosmos all the way up and all the way down.
- ◆ Our intention is to participate in the evolution of love.

   [In the next few pages we will cover some key concepts which are essential to locating ourselves and setting the context for all the One Mountain, Many Paths Oral Essays. —Eds.]

OVERVIEW: EROS IS NO LONGER A LUXURY—IT'S LOVE OR DIE

Eros is life.

The failure of Eros destroys life.

Our lack of Eros is poised to destroy the world.

All civilizations have fallen because the stories that they lived in were, in some sense, stories based on rivalrous conflict governed by win/lose metrics. Every civilization was weakened by interior polarization caused by the lack of a shared Story of Value.

We now have a global civilization, but we haven't created a shared Story of Value.

We haven't solved the generator functions that caused all civilizations to fall. Our global civilization has exponential technologies and extraction models depleting the Earth of resources that took billions of years to create, which is going to lead to a civilizational collapse.

Existential risk is risk to our very existence.

The choice is clear: love or die.

It's that simple.

Eros is no longer a luxury. It is an absolute necessity for the survival of the individual and the planet.

In the last half a century, modern psychology has documented an age-old truth: a fully nourished baby who is not held in loving arms will die.

So too, our world, both personal and global—even with all the resources of intelligence and technology at our disposal—will die without being held in love, in the embrace of Eros.

We must embrace a personal path of love and a global politics of love.

Not ordinary love. Not love which is "mere human sentiment," but Eros, or what we sometimes call Outrageous Love, which is the heart of existence itself.

We live in a world of outrageous pain.

The only response is Outrageous Love.

WHAT IS EROS?

Eros is the experience of radical aliveness, moving towards, seeking, desiring ever-deeper contact and ever-greater wholeness.[4] Eros is the core fabric of Reality's being and the motivational architecture of Reality's becoming.

Eros is what animates the evolutionary impulse itself, from the very inception of Cosmos all the way to our very selves, who awaken to the realization that the evolutionary impulse throbs uniquely in each of us.

The realization of human awakening and transformation that lies at the core of the interior sciences is the invitation—or even the urgent and desperate demand—of a madly loving Cosmos animated by infinities of power and infinities of intimacy.

The demand—the desperate invitation, the plea, the tender and fierce command of Cosmos that lives inside every human being—is to awaken: to awaken to our true nature as unique incarnations of Eros and Ethos that are needed and desperately desired by All-That-Is. Said slightly differently: Reality is Eros. Or: God is Eros.

The failure of Eros destroys life. The collapse of Eros is always the hidden (or not so hidden) root cause for the collapse of ethics.

This is true both personally and collectively. We live in a moment of a worldwide and personal collapse of Eros. Our lack of Eros is poised to destroy

---

4   We define Eros through what we refer to as the Eros equation (one of a series of what we call interior science equations):

Eros = Radical Aliveness × Desiring (Growing + Seeking) × Deeper Contact × Greater Wholeness × Self Actualization/Self Transcendence (Creation [Destruction])

There are good reasons for the formal language of the interior science equations in these writings, and the reader is invited to explore them on their own, in particular, in our work, David J. Temple, *First Principles and First Values: Forty-Two Propositions on CosmoErotic Humanism, the Meta-Crisis, and the World to Come* (World Philosophy and Religion, 2024).

the world. Humanity is currently experiencing what has come to be known as existential risk, a risk to our very existence, or what I will refer to as the Second Shock of Existence.

EXISTENTIAL RISK: THE SECOND SHOCK OF EXISTENCE

The first shock of existence is the death of the human being—the realization that we will die, which dawns in human consciousness at the beginning of history. We are not talking about the biological fact of death but the *existential* realization of death. Although the interior sciences disclose that death is a portal between two days (there is vast empirical,[5] philosophical,[6] and anthro-ontological evidence[7] for the continuity of consciousness[8]), death is also, in our own direct surface experience, a stark end. And that is obviously not a bug, but a feature in the system.

5   We refer to evidence gathered by the most serious of researchers, beginning with Henry and Edith Sedgwick at Cambridge University and William James at Harvard University, and continuing in highly rigorous form for the last 150 years, as recapitulated by Whiteheadian scholar David Ray Griffin in multiple volumes. See also, for example, Dean Radin, *Real Magic: Unlocking Your Natural Psychic Abilities to Create Everyday Miracles* (Potter/TenSpeed/Harmony, 2018), *The Conscious Universe: The Scientific Truth of Psychic Phenomena* (HarperCollins, 2010), and other books. Or see the earlier classic by Frederic William Henry Myers, *Human Personality and Its Survival of Bodily Death* (Longmans, Green, 1907).

6   This requires a cogent analysis of materialism and dualism, and the introduction of the far more cogent third possibility, which we have called "pan-interiority."

7   We discuss Anthro-Ontology in some depth in *First Principles and First Values*, and see also the fuller conversation in David J. Temple, *First Principles and First Values: Towards an Evolving Perennialism: Introducing the Anthro-Ontological Method*—both published by World Philosophy and Religion Press, in conjunction with Integral Publishers. For now, we will simply define it as an "innate and clear interior gnosis directly available to the human being."

8   See Dr. Marc Gafni and Dr. Zachary Stein's essay in preparation, "Beyond Death: Anthro-Ontology, Philosophy, and Empiricism." This essay is slated to appear in the book *Towards a World Religion: Homo Amor Essays*. The essay is also the ground for a larger book by the same authors, *Twelve Portals to Life Beyond Death: Responding to the Second Shock of Existence*, in which we discuss three forms of material: the empirical, the philosophical, and the anthro-ontological, and show how each form discredits the notion of death as the end.

Our first-person experience is that death ends this life. It is not the *totality* of our experience if we go deeper inside, but it is obviously intended to be the central, potent, and painful dimension of every human life. Indeed, as Ernest Becker potently reminded us, the denial of death is at our peril.

All the stories and all the plotlines and all the threads of living end at that moment. Whatever happens beyond, we have an actual experience of ending. **Paradoxically, that ending, the experience of the finality of mortality, is what presses us into life.** From the implicit demand of the first shock of existence, human beings were activated and pressed into creative emergence, and what emerged was all of human culture, both interior and exterior.

The second shock of existence is the realization of the potential death of all humanity. After all the stages of human history—matter, life, and mind in all of their stages of evolutionary unfolding—we have come to this place in the evolution of humanity, in which the gap between our exponentially expanding exterior technologies and our stalled (or even regressing) interior technologies of value has created dire catastrophic and existential risks.

This gap generates extraction models and exponential growth curves, rivalrous conflicts based on win/lose metrics, tragedies of the commons, and multipolar traps, in which everyone has to keep producing to the nth degree, including weaponized exponential threats to our very existence because we are afraid that the other parties are going to do it and not be transparent—hide it from us and then dominate us.

GENERATOR FUNCTIONS FOR EXISTENTIAL RISK

Let's outline clearly the main *generator functions for existential risk*.

Rivalrous conflicts governed by zero-sum, win/lose metrics. Rivalrous conflicts generate extraction models at the core of the economic system and exponential growth curves. Both of these drive and are driven by a contrived system of artificially manufactured desires and needs, delivered into culture by ever more precise forms of micro-targeting to individuals and groups through the ever more immersive environment of the internet.

Next, rivalrous conflicts and exponential growth curves animated by win/lose metrics generate **complicated, fragile world systems** highly vulnerable to myriad forms of collapse. Fragile local systems are made exponentially more fragile on a global level by our inability to meet global challenges with social, legal, political, economic, and ethical infrastructures that remain largely local.

All of this is a direct result of the failure to develop more adequate interior technologies that would be sufficiently compelling to displace "rivalrous conflict governed by win/lose metrics" as the motivational architecture for the human life world.

This failure has led to the conditions that will cause the implosion of systems that are already and quite literally on the brink of collapsing themselves. That's what we mean by the *second shock of existence.*

To recapitulate: the second shock of existence is not the death of the human being, but the potential death of humanity.

It is the *Death Star* moment of our species.

THE DECONSTRUCTION OF INTRINSIC VALUE

We stand in this moment poised between utopia and dystopia, at a time between worlds and a time between stories. We need a new Story of Value, eternal yet evolving, rooted in First Principles and First Values, which would become a universal grammar of value and a context for our diversity.

This is exactly what the Renaissance was. It was a time between worlds and a time between stories. In the Renaissance, we had recently been challenged by the Black Death, a pandemic that swept across Europe. The

Black Death destroyed between a third to half of Europe and a huge part of Asia. People died horrifically, brutally, in the streets. They had no idea how to meet this challenge, and so, in response to the Black Death, da Vinci and Ficino and their cohorts understood that they had to tell a new Story of Value.

That story was the story of modernity. Did they get it right?

- They got part of it right, which birthed, to use Jürgen Habermas' phrase, "the dignities of modernity," such as new ways of gathering information and universal human rights.
- But they also deconstructed the source of Value. They lost the basis for the Good, the True, and the Beautiful.

The basis used to be divine revelation: *God told us.* But this claim was owned by religion, and every religion began to overreach and over-claim. The revelation was thus often mediated through cultural categories and wasn't fully accurate.

Modernity threw out revelation, but was unable to establish a new basis for value.

Value was just assumed to be real. As it says in the founding document of the American Revolution: *We hold these truths to be self-evident*—that is, *we don't really have a basis for value; we just take it as a given.*

In other words, modernity took out a loan of social capital from the traditional world. The source of value was never worked out.

And then, gradually, value began to collapse.

- The Universe Story began to collapse.
- The belief that the Good, the True, and the Beautiful are real began to collapse.
- The belief that Love is real began to collapse.

As Bertrand Russell is reported to have said, "I cannot see how to refute the arguments for the subjectivity of ethical values, but I find myself incapable of believing that all that is wrong with wanton cruelty is that I do not like it."

What do you do if you grew up in a world in which value is not real? A world without a source of value, without a Universe Story, without a story of human identity, without a story of desire, without a narrative of power?

In the words of W.B. Yeats, *the center does not hold.*

- You have a collapse at the very center of society, because you no longer have Eros.
- You no longer have a Reality in which value is real, and so you have this lingering sense of emptiness.
- You have a complete collapse at the very center.
- We become *the hollow men and the stuffed men*, gesture without form.

And that's the source of our current existential risk.

THE DEEPER ROOT CAUSE OF THE META-CRISIS: A GLOBAL INTIMACY DISORDER

Above, I have outlined the major generator functions of existential risk. But there is a deeper cause for the existential risk that lurks underneath the rivalrous conflict governed by win/lose metrics and the fragile systems they engender.

And we cannot take the Death Star down without discerning and addressing this. We have already alluded to this root cause above, but at this point we need to make it more explicit so that, from this context, the adequate root response will become clear.

Modernity threw out the revelation, but was unable to establish a new basis for value.

This ostensibly surprising statement can be understood in a few simple steps:

1. All of the catastrophic and existential risk challenges we face are global: from climate change to artificial intelligence, pandemics, systems collapse, and exponential arms races.
2. Every global challenge self-evidently requires a global solution.
3. Global solutions can only be implemented with global co-ordination.
4. Global co-ordination is impossible without global coherence.
5. Global coherence is only possible if there is a global resonance between the parts.
6. Global resonance is only possible if we have global intimacy.

ONLY A SHARED STORY OF VALUE CAN GENERATE GLOBAL INTIMACY

Global intimacy—just like intimacy in a couple—is only possible when there is a shared story.

Not just a shared history, but a shared Story of Value.

- It is only a shared global story that can generate a new emergent quality of intimacy: global intimacy.
- A shared Story of Value must be rooted in shared ordinating values, or what we have called evolving First Values and First Principles.
- Intimacy requires a shared grammar of value as a matrix for a shared Story of Value.

The global intimacy disorder is the root cause for existential risk. The global intimacy disorder underlies the core generator functions for existential risk.

The global intimacy disorder is rooted in the failure to experience ourselves in a field of shared intrinsic value. This failure derives from the deconstruction of value.

Indeed, it is wholly accurate to say that **the root cause of the two generator functions of existential risk is the failed story of intrinsic value, or what we might also call the breakdown of Eros.**

1. The first generator function is **the success story**. Our modern success story is rivalrous conflict governed by win/lose metrics, which violates all the terms of the Intimacy Equation: there is no shared identity and no mutuality of recognition, feeling, value or purpose, and instead of *relative* otherness, there is *alienated* otherness. Such a story generates complicated fragile systems with no allurement or intimacy between the parts, systems which optimize for efficiency (as an expression of win/lose metrics) and not for resiliency and life.

2. The second generator function is **the deconstruction of intrinsic value** itself. The deconstruction of value is the sense that human value does not participate in the intrinsic value of the Real, for the Real is dogmatically declared to have no intrinsic value. Thus, there is no shared identity between the interior of the human being and Reality. There is no common participation in a field of shared intrinsic value. Instead of being intimate with value, we are alienated from value. And only intrinsic value can arouse will: political, moral, and social will.

To sum up, without a shared grammar of value there is no global intimacy, and therefore no global coherence, and no global coordination in response to catastrophic and existential risk, which means, put simply, there will be, quite literally, no future.

HEALING THE GLOBAL INTIMACY DISORDER
REQUIRES THE EVOLUTION OF INTIMACY

But we are not hopeless. On the contrary, we are filled with great hope. Hope is a memory of the future. That memory of the future *is* the direct hit that takes down the Death Star, the culture of death. **The direct hit must be**—as it has always been in history—**the emergence of a new stage of evolution.**

Crisis is an evolutionary driver, and every crisis is, at its core, a crisis of intimacy: from the oxygen crisis of the single cells dying which generated multicellular life at the dawn of existence, to the existential risk in this very moment.[9]

The direct hit is therefore structurally self-evident: the evolution of intimacy itself.

What is intimacy, as a structure of Cosmos all the way down and all the way up the evolutionary chain? We engage this inquiry in depth in other writings, but for now we will simply adduce what we have called the "Intimacy Equation":

Intimacy = shared identity in the context of [relative] otherness x mutuality of recognition x mutuality of pathos x mutuality of value x mutuality of purpose

Intimacy is about the capacity of parts to generate a *shared identity* while retaining their otherness, or distinct identity. This requires multiple mutualities, including recognition, pathos (or feeling), value, and purpose. The parts must recognize and feel each other, even as they share value and purpose. But all of this must lead to intimate union—and not pathological

---

9 We demonstrate this principle in some depth in the multi-volume series, *The Universe: A Love Story* (forthcoming) (https://worldphilosophyandreligion.org/early-ontologies), *The Intimate Universe: Global Intimacy Disorder as Cause for Global Action Paralysis* (forthcoming), and in other writings of CosmoErotic Humanism.

fusion, where the distinct identity of the parts disappears—like subatomic particles that successfully become an atom, or two people who successfully become a couple.

THE DECONSTRUCTION OF VALUE IS THE DECONSTRUCTION OF INTIMACY

We have identified the global intimacy disorder as the root cause of existential risk. But the underlying ultimate failure of intimacy is the deconstruction of value itself.

The deconstruction of value means that human value does not participate in any sense of intrinsic value of the Real. This is not about individual *values*, but about *the Field of Value* that underlies all of them. **When the human being**—moved, often sincerely or even nobly, by myriad cultural, historical, and psychological confusions—**claims to have stepped out of the Field of Value, then intimacy itself is deconstructed.**

The deconstruction of value is the deconstruction of intimacy.

In the absence of a shared Story of Value, a story that is an authentic expression of Reality's Eros, a story rooted in *pseudo-Eros* takes center stage and becomes the generator function for existential risk. Our modern pseudo-Eros story is *rivalrous conflict governed by win/lose metrics.* Such a story catalyzes in its wake the second generator function of existential risk: *complicated fragile systems with no allurement or intimacy between the parts.* It is in that sense that we have argued that the first generator function for existential risk is the success story.

- ◆ The failure of intimacy is precisely the impotent experience that there is no shared identity between the interior of the human being and Reality. **There is no shared identity in the sense of any kind of common participation in a field of shared intrinsic value.**

- **But only a shared Story of Value can arouse the global will required to engage catastrophic and existential risk.** For it is only global political, moral, and social will—and we can even say *erotic* will—that can generate the most Good, True and Beautiful world that we have always known is possible.

THE EVOLUTION OF LOVE IS THE TELLING OF A NEW STORY

Coupled with the Intimacy Equation is the scientifically grounded realization, in both the exterior and interior sciences, that Reality is a progressive deepening of intimacies, or, said slightly differently:

Reality is Evolution. Evolution is the evolution of intimacy.

- The evolution of intimacy requires—both personally and collectively—a deeper, more accurate discernment of the nature of our universe, ourselves, and our beloveds.
- This new discernment generates a new global Story of Value.
- The new global Story of Value generates an emergent, heretofore unseen global intimacy and heals the global intimacy disorder.

The new Story of Value is the direct hit that takes down the Death Star and replaces it with the hope that invokes the memory of our best future.

Global intimacy facilitates global coherence, which facilitates global coordination, which activates the possibility of our creative and effectively coordinated global responses to the global meta-crisis in its entirety and its specific expressions.

To solve Bertrand Russell's challenge—the apparent argument for the subjectivity of ethical values—**we have to reground value theory in eternal yet evolving First Principles and First Values, and articulate a new Story of Value.**

This is what we call CosmoErotic Humanism.

CosmoErotic Humanism—together with other emergent strands—**needs to become the ground of a world religion as a context for our diversity**. We need religion, even as we need science, to articulate a shared global grammar of value.

As we said at the beginning, our choice is simple: love or die.

- To love means to participate in the evolution of love, which is the evolution of the human Story of Value.
- To love means to evolve and activate a new cultural enlightenment—rooted in a new narrative of identity, a new narrative of value, a new narrative of intimate communion, a new narrative of desire, a new narrative of power—all of which will birth new narratives of economics and politics.
- The evolution of love is the telling of a new Story.

The new Story that must be told is a love story, for in fact that is the deepest truth of Reality, rooted in the best exterior and interior sciences, that we have at this moment in time:

- Reality is not merely a fact. Reality is a story.
- Reality is not an ordinary story. Reality is a love story.
- Reality is not an ordinary love story. Reality is an Outrageous Love Story.

Story doesn't mean it's *made-up*.

It means doing the hard work of integrating the validated insights of the traditional world, the modern world, and the postmodern world.

This is the intention at the heart of telling the new Story of CosmoErotic Humanism.

ABOUT THIS VOLUME

We Are God's Unique Intimacy is a clarion call to revolutionary transformation.

At the heart of this transformation lies a radical insight:

> You are a Unique Self: an irreducibly unique expression of the LoveIntelligence and LoveBeauty that is the animating and initiating Eros and energy of All-That-Is, that lives in you, as you, and through you.[1]

In other words, you are a unique expression of what is often talked about in the Enlightenment traditions as True Self, or the Field of Consciousness that is one with All-That-Is. Your Unique Self is that field having a "you-experience." Therefore, your distinct perspective and your "you-ness" are not accidental, but essential. You are the personal face of the universal, the *LoveIntelligence* and *LoveBeauty* of Cosmos uniquely incarnate as you.

When you offer your *unique Outrageous Acts of Love*—those acts that no one but you can give—you participate directly in the evolution of love itself. These acts are not necessarily heroic in the conventional sense. Sometimes, they're as small as slipping a symbolic note under someone's door that only you can write. These are evolutionary acts. They are your "unique fixing" (your *tikkun*)—your personal role in the repair and evolution of Reality.

---

1   Marc Gafni, *Your Unique Self: the Radical Path to Personal Enlightenment* (2012)

As Unique Selves, we are *allured* to come together to form Unique Self Symphonies. We are allured to each other, because **he entire Cosmos is structured by allurement and amazement.** Allurement is not a metaphor—it is a property of Cosmos. Allurement is the interior experience of gravitational attraction. It is Eros calling to Eros—the evolutionary force of intimacy drawing us toward ever-greater wholeness. Attraction is the visible face of allurement, and allurement is a choice. When we respond to authentic allurement, we deepen intimacy and step into our sacred obligation to evolve.

But we must clarify our Unique Self, to distinguish true allurement from pseudo-allurement, which arises when we seek to fill the hole in our uniqueness rather than live from its fullness.

In this realization, allurement becomes a sacred invitation—part of the very movement of **Evolutionary Love that awakens us to the intimacy, uniqueness, and amazement at the heart of Cosmos.**

So as we said above, when we awaken as Unique Self, we are *allured* to come together in Unique Self Symphony. A Unique Self Symphony is an *omni-considerate* configuration of Unique Selves, each playing their unique instrument for the sake of the whole.

In a *Unique Self Symphony*, we share identity without collapsing into sameness; we generate intimacy not by fusing or erasing our uniqueness but rather *through* our uniqueness.

Separation is the coin of alienation. Uniqueness is the currency of connection.

In CosmoErotic Humanism, intimacy as a First Principle and First Value[2] of Cosmos is formulated as follows:

---

2   David J. Temple, *First Principles and First Values: Forty-two Propositions on CosmoErotic Humanism* (2024).

Intimacy is shared identity in the context of otherness times mutuality of recognition, mutuality of pathos, mutuality of value, and mutuality of purpose.

The evolutionary intimacy of Unique Self Symphony is not metaphor—it's a new structure of Divinity, a new ontology of intimacy, shared identity in the context of uniqueness otherness.

Unique Self Symphony is not just poetic language or symbolic imagery. Rather, it refers to a real, ontological structure of Reality—a new structure of intimacy. In which unique selves gather into a unique *we,* each playing their unique instrument even each instrument unique plays the same musical score—the shared music of the whole.

Therefore, this vision also invites us to step into a new realization of *the Divine.* First, we are invited to know *God as the Infinity of Power.* We reclaim power as sacred, rooted not in domination but in desire, because "your desire is evolution's desire." To reclaim power is to affirm our capacity to participate in the re-patterning of Reality. We not only live in the intimate universe; the intimate universe lives in us. As such, the whole lives in us, even as we live in the whole. And as such, we have the capacity to re-pattern, to transform, and to evolve the whole.

As we evolve from false humility or victimhood, we realize that our power is the power of the whole itself uniquely incarnate in us, as us, and through us.

This is not the coercive power of win/lose metrics, but the evolutionary power of standing in integrity and taking our unique risk.

In this new realization, we recognize that *we are God's unique intimacy of power,* called to infuse technological, cultural, and personal power with the Eros of Evolutionary Love.

But God is not only the Infinity of Power—God is also the Infinity of Intimacy.

Indeed, in CosmoErotic Humanism we whisper the name of God, we call the name of God as the Infinite Intimate.

God is intimate with us—not as a distant force or abstract principle, but as the personal face of Cosmos who knows our name. Even as God is *wholly other*, *mysterium tremendum*, and beyond all names.

The sacred nature of the Divine is the dialectic between radical intimacy and radical otherness. To know that "God is intimate with me" is to realize that I am not a separate self in an alien universe, but a unique incarnation of the Intimate Universe itself.

- You are not just in relationship to God, you are God's *unique intimacy*.
- You are a unique incarnation of the Intimate Universe.
- Your very existence is a unique expression of the Divine.
- Your desire is the desire of God moving through you.

So, when two Unique Selves meet, their unique intimacy creates a new resonance in the Field. That resonance is not just a new frequency of relationship. It is a new frequency of Divinity itself. It is a new configuration of intimacy.

Indeed, Unique Self Symphony is a new configuration of intimacy in which Unique Selves join genius to fulfill their evolutionary obligation. To participate in the evolution of love. To write a new chapter in the Love Story of Cosmos.

Because your unique intimacy is not separate from the Cosmos. Your intimacy participates in the evolution of love itself. Your intimacy participates in the unfolding of Evolution: The Love Story of the Universe.

Reality is not a fact, Reality is a story. Reality is not static. Reality is not a closed system. Reality is evolutionary. Reality has directionality. That directionality is not arbitrary. Evolution is not random, but is the progressive deepening of intimacy. The trajectory of Cosmos—what we call Evolutionary Love—is towards ever deeper union, all the way up and all the way down the evolutionary chain, from atoms to galaxies, from cells to culture. Reality has a plotline.

The Universe is not a fact—it is a *Love* Story. But not ordinary love. The Universe is an Outrageous Love Story. Outrageous Love is the love that moves the sun and the stars. It is the initiating and animating Eros of Reality itself. Outrageous Love is the evolutionary impulse awake and alive in you, as you, and through you.

And it is this evolutionary impulse that calls us now to awaken as *Homo amor*—the fulfillment of *Homo sapiens*—each of us a unique configuration of intimacy, irreducibly needed and desired by All-That-Is, to participate directly in the healing and transformation of Reality.

Volume 6

These oral essays are edited talks delivered by Marc Gafni and Barbara Marx Hubbard between October and December 2017.

CHAPTER ONE

FOLLOW THE IMPULSE AND PLAY A LARGER GAME

Episode 51—October 14, 2017

EVOLUTIONARY LOVE CODE: UNIQUE SELF AS EXPRESSION OF TRUE SELF

Your Unique Self is the unique expression of your True Self.

The total number of True Selves in the world is one. We are all part of The One. Your awakening takes place when you realize that you are not merely a separate self, but True Self. True Self is the singular that has no plural, it is True Self plus your unique perspective.

Unique perspective means the perspective which you are seeing from, and it means your unique intimacy.

Wow, the word intimacy. So, your Unique Self is your unique intimacy with yourself, and the deepest evolutionary impulse expressed uniquely as you.

Tune in to True Self who is one with All.

Your True Self.

One with All.

Feeling yourself to be a member of this whole planetary body which is your True Self in its awesome complexity

and greatness, who is now awakening as a Unique Self and a unique expression of the True Self, which is one with the whole. You are both *one-with-All* and a *unique-one-with-All-That-Is.*

Feel into this resonant field. Tune into your unique expression, intimately one with the True Self of All. Feel how this is coming forth, empowered to give it all, without having to separate ourselves from each other.

PLAYING A LARGER GAME FOR THE EVOLUTION OF LOVE

The invitation in this resonant field is symphonic movements. We resonate in the symphony, and when we resonate, it gets bigger and it gets larger. We invite a particular resonance. We're not just seeking to have a good experience, although we're all about having a good experience. We are all about feeling good, feeling good in the deepest sense of the pleasure of evolution arising in us.

But we are doing so much more, because **the ultimate feel-good is to participate together in the evolution of love**. What we are doing, holy brothers and sisters from around the world, is:

We are participating together
in the evolution of love.

We are doing that by enacting and scribing and bringing down together the evolutionary codes.

In our resonance together we are creating the evolutionary codes which we want to offer into humanity as the best evolution of the source code, the best Universe Story, the best story of identity available today.

We are working together to awaken humanity, to become the new human, to become the New Humanity.

We are doing what they did in the Renaissance, when da Vinci gathered with his friends in Florence, or what they did in Bethlehem, or what they did in Beirut at a particular time when the Sufis were coming together there: creating the best nightlife that Beirut ever knew.

We are *the ones*. It is our turn. We are participating in the evolution of love.

The invitation that we issue to ourselves, that we all issue to each other, all over the world, is the question: *are we ready to play a larger game?*

> *Are we ready to play a larger game? Are we ready to participate in the evolution of love?*

PRAYER AND THE PARTICIPATION IN GOD

We begin always with prayer. We begin with the evolution of prayer. We pray not to the Santa Claus god who demands our emasculation and obedience. We pray to the God who *holds* us, not just who *is* us. We don't pray to that old New Age narcissism-god: *God is us,* and that is the end of the story. No, no, no—God is *beyond* us. I didn't create photosynthesis. You didn't manifest mitosis and meiosis. You and I are great, but mitosis and meiosis lived before any of us.

So, it's about the LoveIntelligence of Reality *that holds us*!

To know that every place we fall, we fall into Her hands. We call Her sometimes, *She*, God/Goddess, we call Her the Tao, we call her the Way. We call Her the LoveIntelligence and the LoveBeauty of all of Reality that infuses Reality with meaning, purpose in every second. **At the same time—in the great paradox—that very LoveIntelligence lives *in* us, *as* us, and *through* us.**

The code that we are going to talk about is the knowing that **we are not only held by God, but that we *participate* in God.** We are not only *held*

3

by the Field, but the entire Field *lives as us.* That is not a metaphor and that is not a dogmatic claim. That is the lived reality of the awakened human being.

How do we have an experience of democratized enlightenment? When we know that our Unique Self is not just my Myers-Briggs test, but this code:

My Unique Self is the unique expression of my True Self.

When we pray, who do we pray to? Well, we pray to *the Field.* But is the Field impersonal? No, it is not just *the Force* in *Star Wars,* although George Lucas was pointing toward something when he talked about *the Force,* because he realized God is not just Santa Claus, it is the Force: *May the Force be with you!*

But now put Santa Claus together with *the Force* and then put a little Kali in from Hinduism. Put the most beautiful, tender, and the most audacious, awake, sensual, alive personal experience you ever had, and you have a sense of *the Force.*

The Force is the Infinity of Intimacy which is fervent and creative. It is throbbing, it is pulsating, it is dripping with aliveness. It is totally personal, and it is totally beyond personal.

God is the Infinity of Intimacy that knows my name.

She addresses us personally: *Hey you, are you sitting in front of that altar? And you, are you there? And what's going on with you there in New Mexico, were you waking up this morning? How is it over there with you in France? Hello, how is Holland? What's going on in Bedford?*

Like, oh my god, that Infinity of Intimacy that knows our name and cares tenderly, passionately, infinitely, with utter delight, with utter devotion. And here is the next sentence: with utter *demand.* **With utter delight, and utter demand, and utter devotion, the Infinity of Intimacy says: *Oh my***

4

god, your life matters so much to me! You are not alone, I am with you, I am sitting by your bedside. I am sitting with you at work, and I am watching everything you do. I am holding you accountable and I am infusing myself in you. I need you.

You are part of the True Self. **You are part of the field, and the field is absent and deficient without you.**

We turn to that Infinity of Intimacy that is the personal God, but not the small personal god. It is not the cosmic vending-machine personal god, hijacked by one religion which says, *put in the coin,* which is my prayer, *and get out a shiny car.*

It is the Infinity of Intimacy that suffuses all of Reality, that knows our name and holds us in every moment. Oh my God, dearest, most beloved friends, honored colleagues, honored friends, what a delight to know that I am held in every moment.

You know that the LoveIntelligence that manifested mitosis and meiosis manifested every single one of us—every one of us.

We bring our prayers before *that* God because the god we don't believe in doesn't exist. **We bring the good news of our lives before *that* God, who is the Infinity of Intimacy.** We bring the stories of our lives, our *holy and our broken Hallelujahs,* and we realize we are not separate from the field. We *are* the field, and every breath we draw is *Hallelujah,* is the field itself, is pristine praise, is the glory of God. We can reclaim those words: *The glory of God.* **And we know that *God is us, God holds us, God knows us,* and God is more personal than anything we can imagine.**

We are resetting the source code of evolution itself as we offer our prayers, asking God for everything. We evolve the source code together and offer our prayers, because prayer affirms the dignity of personal need. When we pray we say, *help me! Help me to have enough funds to give my gift into the world! Help my uncle, help my daughter to get the right treatment this week.*

We ask for everything because prayer affirms the dignity of personal need.

Remember, we cannot change the world if we don't pray. Communism, the great changer of the world, forgot to pray. It killed more people than any other force in history. Prayer means I am partnering with God. And God cares about every detail. I offer my prayer and I know that I am held. Oh my God! Let's offer our prayers, let's testify together. Pray for details! Don't skip the details of your life—it is a bypass! Find your truest desire.

Your desire is evolution's desire.

Your unrest is the blessed unrest of evolution itself.

Find your desire!

As we pray, we blow it open. When we pray, we impress our lips on the heart of the Divine, the Infinity of Intimacy that knows our name and manifested everything. And She waits for our prayer, because **when we articulate our prayer, we find the deepest depth of our own need.** And we ask for everything, because we know that if our needs are not met, the field is deficient. And when we don't love ourselves, we are narcissists.

Self-love means our needs matter, our dignity matters. Once our dignity matters and we stand for our dignity, only then can we stand for the dignity of All-That-Is. No one is degraded. No one is outside of the circle.

We lead with compassion.

We lead with appreciation.

We lead with awakening as True Self that is One.

A PLANETARY AWAKENING IN LOVE THROUGH
UNIQUE SELF SYMPHONIES

And here is our ultimate prayer:

We pray for a Planetary Awakening in Love through a Unique Self Symphony.

This entire planet, with all its members, is awakening in some way to this exact experience of being an expression of the impulse of evolution as love. The entire planet! Well, why not? Because it is *so*!

How many people does it take to make something *so*, by knowing it is *so*? We don't know, but if we are in this big field (and most people don't really know this, but *we* do), to the degree we are *strong in our knowing* we are affecting the entire planetary organism. Why? Because it is one planetary body.

A planetary awakening in love through a Unique Self Symphony, what does that mean?

Each of us is a Unique Self. It is a big job to get to that realization. You are not born knowing this, but each of us *is that*, so we recognize it even if we don't know it all the time.

Coming together as Unique Self Symphony means that my voice, your voice, every voice on this planet is awakened to the reality of **being a participant in the planetary birth.**

How many of those awake voices are there? Well, not quite enough, yet.

But every single person who says *Yes* to this, who goes out into the world as that *Yes*, matters infinitely. Everywhere, every one of us is saying the internal *Yes*: I am a True Self, part of the whole body as an intimate, unique expression of it. **If you hold that in your being, everywhere you go, people wake up—just because of you.**

FOLLOW THE IMPULSE!

I want to tell a brief story here and ask you to share it with me to clarify the process of participation in the planetary birth, because almost none of us were born with this awareness. There was no religion for it. There was no culture.

I remember one of my first memories: I (Barbara) was born in 1929. I remember at about the age of six, saying to my parents, *you know what? This isn't normal! The entire world!* The way it was you know— competition, winning, the war, the horrors, asking: *Is this normal?* And then I can remember thinking, *well, how do I know that? What is normal?* Deep inside I knew it was not that. I began to search in some strange way after we dropped the atomic bombs on Japan. That was super not normal to be at the threshold of destroying the entire world. I realized, maybe *somebody* knows what is normal. Somebody who could answer the question of how to use all the power that is good. I decided I am going to try to go to church.

Do you know this? **Did you ever wake up saying, *this isn't quite normal?***

Just remember it for a moment. What did it feel like to ever wake up and think, *wow, is all this violence normal*?

Did you ever feel that?

As I felt it, being a sort of pioneering soul, I decided to find out who knows what is normal. So, I joined the Episcopal Church in Scarsdale, New York, and I asked the minister, *is any of this true, any of it in the Bible, that Jesus did this, taught this, died, was resurrected, et cetera? We will do the same—wow, that's good news, right there. Is that normal?* And he said, *young lady, you go to Sunday school.* So, I went to Sunday school at the Episcopal Church in Scarsdale, New York, and I asked again: *Is any of this true?* Of course, nobody knew, nobody cared, nobody thought so. They might have thought it somewhere deep inside. But to say, *it's really true*—No!

Just think about yourself. What search did you have to go on to pick up this book?

I was not only asking that question in the Episcopal Church, I also asked it in university. How many of you went to university, or college, or to any educational world, and you asked the question:

---

*What is my unique purpose
in a world that is awakening
to its full potential?*

Did you get any class on that anywhere? No!

I went to Bryn Mawr College, and I remember asking the question in some French class—I was asking wherever I could, **what is the direction of our humanity and how can I help it get there?** They would say to me, *young lady, this is the French class. Young lady, this is the philosophy class.* I got no answer. So, I just decided to find out myself.

This is something we all need to do if we want to participate in a planetary awakening in love.

At Bryn Mawr College, which was supposed to be a good university, you could not even take a class on why we are here, or where we are going, or the direction of evolution.

This is still the case.

I was really, frustrated. I will not go through my entire life, but I will tell you what happened to make it possible for me to be sitting here with you.

I met a man at a little café in the Left Bank in Paris. This was during the time after the Second World War when the feeling to be helpful, hopeful, was considered stupid. This was in France after what they suffered. I asked this young artist man, who was sitting opposite me, *what is your purpose?* And he said, *I am an artist seeking a new image of man commensurate with our power to shape the future.*

See! This is important for everyone. **Do you remember when you got a clue of why you are here?**

When this young man said, *I am an artist seeking a new image of man commensurate with our power.* **I knew that was my purpose.** I had sensed it before, but I could not have said it until he said it. And I just said internally, *I am going to marry you!* And I did.

When did you get a signal from someone, or something, or some book, that this is your purpose, and you were able to go for it?

I went for it. I got married. I moved to Lakeville, Connecticut. I hated it. I wanted to go to New York and get a job. I mean, I did not do any of the things that I thought I wanted to do. But, I followed my purpose.

Here is the key that then made it possible for me to incarnate it as who I am.

When I got married, I thought, *it is only my husband, I will just support him.* It was before the women's movement. Not after long, I got miserable, I got depressed, I got sick, but nevertheless I picked up the book of Teilhard de Chardin, the French philosopher and paleontologist. He had traced the story of evolution as a rise of consciousness, or awareness, from a single-celled animal to a multi-cellular animal to a human.

- The first quality of evolution was: the **rise of consciousness**.
- The next quality of evolution was: the **rise of freedom**, to do right and to do wrong. Freedom does not mean you always do right.
- The third quality was: **social connectivity**, or evolution of love, through joining together in the greater whole to make the planetary reality.

When I read that, I realized, *oh, that is what I was looking for!* And here was the big insight: not only did Teilhard de Chardin say that, not only could other people say that, but it was already *internalized as me.*

I wanted more **consciousness**.

I wanted more **freedom**.

I wanted more **love**.

And with that *yes,* he gave us a goal. He said, *when the noosphere, the thinking layer of Earth*—which is now social media—*gets its collective eyes. When that happens, there will be the Christification of the Earth* and what we are calling a planetary awakening in love.

What I did at the age of 33, with my five children, and uncertain in so many ways, even of being a woman, I said, *I am going to help do that.* With that, saying, *I am going to help do that,* I was completely awakened. I want to say in conclusion, the goal of everybody who is part of this movement is exactly what woke up in me then.

Follow the evolutionary impulse!

This Reality is something to give thanks for, holding the goal of evolution, offering a container **for the crisis of birth of the Unique Selves everywhere.**

This is not only what we are doing, but what is happening through us.

Why? Because it is natural.

THE INCONSOLABLE LONGING TO PLAY A LARGER GAME

What is True Self? That is the question we are asking here. What is True Self? That is our code. What is True Self? Why is True Self important?

True Self is the field. And the field is awake and alive.

- How do I know that the field is awake and alive?
- How do I know I am not merely a unique set of talents, which is not what Unique Self is?

- How do I know I am a unique expression of the field?
- How do I know that the answer to the question *who you are* is that you are a unique expression of the LoveIntelligence and LoveBeauty, you are the Field of LoveIntelligence, LoveBeauty?
- How do I know it is not just somebody's personal story kind of working out, someone's pathology someplace?
- How do we know it is the field?

We know it is the field **because we experience in ourselves this inconsolable longing to play a larger game**. C. S. Lewis called it an *inconsolable longing* to step up and give a gift that is needed by All-That-Is.

It might be a project but is deeper than a project. It is: **All-That-Is needs you to step up and sing the song that is only yours to sing, or to write the poem that is only yours to write—to do the deed that is Reality's need.** The *yearning* to do the deed that is Reality's need. That yearning is what tells me that I am part of True Self. That I am not separate. It is that Field of Consciousness that asks the *question,* the *quest* that I am on, and says, *I want to participate and play, and I want to be a superhero. I want to be Wonder Woman and Superman. I want to change the whole thing!* And **that is not grandiosity, that is the truest index of my truest nature**.

And to know that it's not a grand, distorted, overweening ambition, but our desire to manifest together the home of the new human and the new humanity, where **we awaken as Outrageous Lovers, and we commit Outrageous Acts of Love that are uniquely needed by All-That-Is.**

We do step into the field and articulate the vision of a conscious evolution.

We do step out of the old structures of lineage to articulate Unique Self and the Universe: A Love Story.

We do join genius.

We will be in the humblest sense of the word *evangelists*[1]—meaning bringing the *good news* that our gifts matter, that our gifts are needed, and that we can create a bottom-up, self-organizing universe in which **our gift changes the whole story**, in which our life becomes the minor fluctuation point that jumps the entire system to a higher level of stasis and equilibrium.

It is the only way to go, and there is no other path:

- There is no top-down path.
- There is no corporate path.
- There is no government path.

All those have value. Corporations have value, governments have value, but we can see clearer than ever that it is **only a rising of Unique Self Symphonics in love**—not an ordinary love, not a love that is a strategy of the ego—but Outrageous Love that **can make it all work.**

HASIDIC STORY OF YOSELLE THE HOLY MISER

I (Marc) am going to tell you a story. I want to tell you a short story.

It is about a man who had, about a week ago, what is called a *yahrzeit*, in one tradition. Some of you may recognize the word, meaning he had the anniversary of his death. It is a story about this man, and he is such a beautiful man, and I love him so much.

His name was Yoselle. He lived in the town of Krakow in the sixteenth century. And in the town of Krakow, people were so poor at the time, and Yoselle was very wealthy. So people used to come to him, and they would say, *Yoselle, can you help us?*

He would never help anyone. And children threw stones at him as he walked through the street because he separated himself from the community. He

---

1   From εὐάγγελος (*euángelos*, "bringing good news")—εὖ (*eû*, "well") + ἀγγέλλειν (*angéllein*, "to announce").

refused—although he had fortunes, gobs of money—he refused to help anyone.

Yoselle was very old, and he was dying. The community came to him and said, *we are going to bury you in the cemetery, but only if you give some donation to the community. You'll help other people before you die.* He said, *no way, I lived alone. I'll die alone.* And he threw them out. He dies the next day, and no one will bury him because he just lived this separate self life. That is what it looked like. He refused to help anyone, you know, and his body just sat there in Krakow, in Poland in the sixteenth century. And no one would bury him, until a neighbor came late at night and quickly buried him.

But then, my friends—and this is one of our core sacred stories in Evolutionary Church—then it was Friday morning and there was a knock on the door of the house of the rabbi in Krakow. And a very poor man said, *Rabbi, could I borrow ten kopeks to prepare for the Sabbath this week?*

The rabbi said, *Well, of course.* And he gives him ten kopeks and he says, *but where were you last week and the week before? Why do you need money now? You have never come to me.* He said, *well, every week until now I would get on Friday morning a little envelope under my door with ten kopeks, and this week I didn't get it.* The rabbi said, *well, it is sort of strange.* But he forgot about it until about three minutes later, there was another knock at the door and there stood a poor woman. And she says, *Rabbi, I have two children. Could I have 15 kopeks this week to borrow from you to prepare for Sabbath and food for my children?* The rabbi said, *Of course, and he gives her 15 kopeks, but where were you last week?* And she says, *well, you know I used to get an envelope under my door with 15 kopeks.* And then there is another knock on the door and another poor man says, *could you give me 19 kopeks? But where were you last week?*

And it is the same story until the house fills up with poor people each asking for 15 or 20 kopeks, and they all remember the same story. A story within a story. What happened? Well, each one tells something similar, each one says something like. . .

14

Well, it was like 20 years ago, and I was so destitute, and I was so poor, and I knew that Yoselle wouldn't give me anything, ever. But I had no money at all and so I went to his house, and I knocked on his door, kind of late at night so no one would see me and how desperate I was. And I was so surprised because Yoselle opened the door. He welcomed me in, and he set me down, and he gave me a schnapps, and he gave me some cake, and he asked me about myself, and all about my life situation. And finally, you know, he said how much would you really need every week to get by? And I would tell him ten kopeks, 17 kopeks, 15 kopeks. And as soon as I would say the amount of money, Yoselle would turn white with rage, and he would say, I can't believe you dare to ask me for money! He was really strong and big, and he'd pick me up, whether I was a man or a woman, and he'd throw me out in the middle of the night. I was so ashamed and so embarrassed that I went to Yoselle, and all of that, I never told anyone. A week or two later, I just blocked it from my mind. And I never put together that seven months later, or eight months later, I started getting an envelope under my door.

And what did Yoselle do? Wow! Wow!

And the rabbi realized, oh my God, *we never knew who was in front of us!*

Because you never know who is awakening as part of the field in giving their gift. And it is not the person who has the big internet site. And it is not the person who is running for president. **It is all the people who are living their lives and giving their gifts with such audacity and such courage.**

And the rabbi realizes, *we refused to even bury Yoselle!*

So, he gathers the whole community, and they go to the synagogue and they pray, and they say, *Yoselle, forgive us! Forgive us!* And they are in the middle of this ecstatic prayer, and the rabbi faints, and he ascends to heaven. And he meets Yoselle there in heaven, and he says, *Yoselle, forgive us! Forgive us! Forgive us!*

And Yoselle said, *no, it is totally okay. I chose my life. I wanted my life.* I wanted to live anonymously. And I wanted to give those gifts without anyone knowing. And don't worry, when I came to be buried—even though you didn't bury me—Lao Tse, and the Buddha, and Moses, and Christ, and the disciples, and Confucius, and the Indian Cherokee elders, they were all here. They all buried me together. I had the most amazing funeral that you could possibly imagine!

And the rabbi said, *Yoselle, Yoselle, how is it for you in heaven?*

And Yoselle said, *well, there is just one thing, I miss Friday morning so much where I got to put envelopes with ten kopeks and 15 kopeks under people's doors.*

THE FIELD AWAKENS THROUGH UNIQUE ACTS OF OUTRAGEOUS LOVE

Oh, my god, friends, each of us, **that is what it means to awaken as the unique expression of True Self.**

True Self, the total number of True Selves in the world is one. But one is *echad*, one, in Hebrew. But *echad* also means *yichud*—utterly unique. The same word in Hebrew for True Self—*echad* is *yichud*—total uniqueness.

The field is *you*-ness, the Field of True Self is having a *you-experience*.

And there are notes with five kopeks that only *you* can slip under someone's door. And **there are notes that only each one of us can slip under someone's door**. My friends, there are notes waiting for all of us. Notes with ten-kopek envelopes that we can slip under someone's door.

We think that being the unique expression of the field means that we must be famous. We think it means that everyone is reading our book and yes, sometimes that is the thing to do, and I believe in writing books as my unique expression. And I'm committed to putting out five books in co-authorship, in one voice. I'm committed to putting out an entire new evolutionary library. And some of us are writing gorgeous books, and others are manifesting a Mystery School. It is all happening.

But you know what my friends? That is not what it is about. **That is just the exterior manifestation for some people in some stories.**

The real story is that I have an envelope and there is someone who needs my envelope. And I am the only one that ever was, is, or will be, that can slip that envelope under their door on Friday morning and know that they need exactly 13 kopeks.

The Field of Outrageous Love only awakens when I commit my unique acts of Outrageous Love that all of Reality needs me to commit. That no one that ever was, is, or will be, can ever commit, but me.

Oh my God, and when we do that together, we form a Planetary Awakening in Love through Unique Self Symphonies. When we all become Yoselle. You know what the Yoselle story is about, my friends?

You never know who someone is.

There are marvelous, beautiful people out there in the world, but your job is not to be those people. Your job is to be you, and slipping a note under someone's door is as influential as writing a best-seller spiritual book. That is true.

Know your karma and then know your *dharma*! And know that no one else can meet it. You never know who someone is, you never know, you never know, you never know!

The thing that's unique with us, along with all the Unique Selves in the entire world saying *Yes*, is the sense that the world itself is giving birth to something new. In this phase of human history, we hear that the world is going down and start to believe it because everybody is telling that story. But we need to hear that the world has massive potential through our Unique Selves. This is not being told!

The key is that everybody is giving their gift. **It is the Unique Self in the unique direction of this larger goal that makes for a catalyst that never existed before.** Unique Self Symphony, a planetary awakening in love through Unique Self Symphony. That is the shared agreement.

Amen.

CHAPTER TWO

YOUR UNIQUE OUTRAGEOUS ACTS OF LOVE MATTER

Episode 52—October 21, 2017

EVOLUTIONARY LOVE CODE: WHO YOU ARE

You are an irreducibly unique expression of the LoveIntelligence and LoveBeauty that is the animating and initiating Eros and energy of All-That-Is, that lives in you, as you, and through you.

Your unique Outrageous Act of Love is happening in the Field of Evolution.

INSTANTANEOUS MANIFESTATION THROUGH INTENTION

Let's understand our ability to resonate and to manifest—you are an irreducibly unique expression.

Just get really in with me and see this:

You are an irreducibly unique expression of the LoveIntelligence and LoveBeauty that is the animating and initiating Eros and energy of All-That-Is, that lives in you, as you, and through you.

We *not only believe* this, but we also *experience* it. I am speaking as exactly this, as my irreducible, infinitely intelligent LoveIntelligence. This is who I am, and I say: *I, LoveIntelligence, will lift you, each one of you personally, over the quantum jump into the quantum potential field, where there is instantaneous connectedness and manifestation through intention.*

Let's *be* that Loveintelligence in the quantum field, which is the field of evolution where intention creates, and recognize that—speaking first of our *shared intention* of a planetary awakening—**by each of us intending it, and by intending it together** in this church, we expect instantaneous manifesting in Reality. That does not mean just one big final event. It means that by intending this right now **we are affecting the planetary awakening.**

Through manifesting the LoveIntelligence as Evolutionary Lovers, through each one of us, **we are manifesting power.** We manifest by doing our unique work and intending it in this quantum field of evolutionary Reality.

I am thinking of the example of Jesus when he said, *Lazarus, arise!* Impossible act! *Lazarus arise, get up and walk!* That is instantaneous manifestation through deep Evolutionary Love intention.

With that power of our intention in mind, we are praying to empower each one of us, to **come alive in that sense of instantaneous intention in the moment**, making Reality *so* for us and eventually for the larger world.

ONLY YOU KNOW IF YOU ARE GIVING YOUR UNIQUE GIFT

Oh my God, I cannot believe that we have the privilege of generations, the privilege of convening the next momentous leap in evolution, the next leap in evolution. When our friend Peter Diamandis[2] talks about *a billion rising*, what Peter gets is the power of the next great wave of the internet. What Peter doesn't get is that it's not *just* about new technologies.

---

2   Peter Diamandis, serial entrepreneur, futurist, technologist, founder of 25 companies.

New technologies by themselves are neutral. It is the interior; it is the Outrageous Love that we pour into the technology that is convening the next momentous leap in evolution. It is the billion rising, committed to and ecstatic about writing evolutionary codes.

We are saying, oh my God, we're in Florence, where da Vinci was together with his friends to bring in modernity out of premodernity. We are in Bethlehem where people came together and said, oh my God, we must move beyond paganism. There is a new vision of intimacy and integrity in the world.

We are at this moment where we are teetering on the brink, when the forces of dissolution, deconstruction, and destruction, when failures of intimacy—because all evil is a failure of intimacy—when the forces that are non erotic are so prevalent. **Eros means the moving towards larger wholes, the move towards contact and larger wholes, creativity, depth, and transformation.**

Non-erotic living is painful. Fracture. Fragment. Separation.

Let's make America great! There is no world today in which we can make *only* America great. America must be great. I am a patriot, let's make America great. And let's make Bulgaria great, and let's make Uganda great. We here are responsible for America. But America can't be great if Uganda is not great. It is one world. And it is one love.

We are resonating in our code that we are going to take into prayer:

You are an irreducible unique expression of the LoveIntelligence and LoveBeauty of All-That-Is.

This means this LoveIntelligence, this Outrageous LoveIntelligence, is living in you. Outrageous LoveIntelligence has a quality of *you-ness,* and it watches you, *every move you make, every breath you take, She is watching you.*[3] She is in you, and *you-ness* can be Outrageous Love in a way that someone else, who is awesome in a different way, who has his own unique awesome contribution to make, can't do!

Here is the story: *You think you made your contribution because you got recognized and got awards.* Here is the holy secret: **Only you know whether you are really giving that gift.** You can get away with it with everyone, but inside yourself you know. The only question is:

Am I committing the Outrageous Acts of Love that evolution needs me to create?

Ramana Maharshi, the great Eastern mystic says: *The great inquiry question is, who are you?*

As we are joining our impulse with delight, we are saying: *The question is not quite, who are you,* in the sense of *I am,* but—are you ready for this?— the question is:

* What does evolution want to *do* through me in this moment? That is the evolutionary question.
* What does evolution want to *feel* through me, in this moment?
* What *act of love* does evolution want to *commit through me,* in this moment?

When I wake up and I know that, in this very moment, evolution has Outrageous Acts of Love, of being, feeling, doing, experiencing, that can only happen through me, and I can't be you. I let that go. And I say:

---

3   Alluding to "Every Breath You Take," a song by The Police, 1983.

Oh my God, I just met you, oh you are awesome. I am in devotion, I am in delight, because I am not trying to be you. And I am not trying to own you. And I am not trying to hijack you. I am in devotion to you. And then, we can be so much more!

That is when whole mates come together, when they are in devotion to each other. Wow.

Some of us recently went to the wedding of a couple of dear friends. We were all in devotion to the emergence, and we all were there together along with this kind of crazy, beautiful, lineage musician. We all came together, and we were in devotion to the Unique We, which is this incarnation of She, expressed by this particular bride and groom that never was, is, or will be, ever again.

WHAT DO WE DO IN PRAYER?

What we say in prayer is: We say, *oh my God, you have Outrageous Acts of Love that no one who ever was, is, or will be, can do but you,* and the entire story of your life, including **every holy and every broken *Hallelujah* was always *Hallelujah*. It was always the weave of evolution.** To allow you to feel, to give, to live, to write, to be, to see in a way that evolution could do only through you. This is the way we are going to awaken the new species. We are about becoming the new human and evolving the new humanity standing for that possibility of possibility. This is the core of the whole thing, of everything—this is the most exciting thing on planet Earth. **This is liberation!** The knowing, that the only person that Reality can be, the only person who it needs to *be through,* and *give its gift through,* is me.

- Evolution *wants me* to say something.
- Evolution *wants you* to say something.
- Evolution *wants me* to listen.
- Evolution *wants all of us* to bring our holy and our broken *Hallelujah,* and everything that is broken in our

lives, and everything that is holy, and to bring it before
God, and to say: *It is all Hallelujah.*

We are going to offer our prayers and we will pray for our personal lives,
the lives of our friends, and we are going to ask for everything—the holy
and the broken *Hallelujah*. **The future is here. Reality waits for us. We
open our hearts.** Thank you, thank you, thank you. *Amen.*

Let our prayers rip! Let our prayers impress on the lips of God. God desires
our prayer.

We pray for everyone. We *are* prayer. We pray for every detail of our life
because prayer affirms the dignity of personal need. When we bring our
broken and our holy *Hallelujah,* we realize, *every breath we drew was
Hallelujah.* We will raise it together.

All the prayers are welling up. We are thinking that God is in every one of
us as Unique Self saying *yes.* We are bringing God in, and we are living God
as the Evolutionary Unique Self.

**What does an Evolutionary Lover do? What does an Outrageous Lover
do?**

Let's first remember: what is an Outrageous Lover? Just think of that
evolutionary core of the spiral going on for the billions and billions of years
to create more complex and loving systems in you and as your Unique
Self. That is to say, **nobody else has that particular impulse of evolution.**
It is Outrageous Love coursing through evolution. It is so different from
normal love. The Big Bang is different from a normal love affair. *Boom! Oh
well, let's create a universe!*

**The Outrageous Love of the origin of evolution is outrageously
magnificent, outrageously intelligent, awesomely creative, beyond,
beyond belief. That fragment is in you.** Andrew Cohen used to say that
there is a constant Big Bang going on in each one of us, when we say *Yes* to
that Outrageous Love in ourselves.

First of all, that's about us all saying *Yes* to whatever that unique impulse is. The second great thing about this is: **Do you suppose that God, Outrageous Lover personified, would like to see you realize your Outrageous Acts of Love?** Or is God neutral? Or does God not care as to how well you will realize that unique Outrageous Lover in unique expression? Here is what we feel:

God not only cares. It is God's passionate love affair having created you as the God Self, that you are, to be as glorious and as full as anything that is possible. In other words: the God in you is working completely with your choice to say *Yes*. This is so important! If we have Outrageous Love to express, and we don't feel potent, it is very easy to say: *Who am I to say Yes to this outrageous yearning I have?*

God says, *I love your outrageous longing to go the whole way. I love your absolutely fabulous desire to bring those memes into Reality. I love your desire that there shall be a collective, and we all come together, each one of us.*

I declare that the God in me is one hundred percent activated to fulfill my unique Outrageous Act of Love. **In the deepest sense, it is God's act through Unique Self.** True Self is the one Field of God-presence. That **True Self is coming out uniquely as Unique Self**, holding the uniqueness of the Divine specifically as you, which it cannot do if you are staying as a True Self and you don't take your part in the puzzle.

Let's say we are each taking that part in the puzzle. Let's say each one is giving an unqualified *Yes* to the uniqueness. We are feeling in it the Outrageous Love affair of the Universe itself animating us.

I, Barbara, can say from deep personal experience that when I lose track of that uniqueness and I am not sure how to express it, I find myself getting tired and distressed and depressed, but the minute I find it again, all that is gone.

How do I find it? Through the compass of joy! **The Unique Self is expressed through the compass of joy. When you express it, you not only feel**

joyful, but every cell in your body is being animated by the God force and you probably start extending your life. We reach what Ray Kurzweil calls *longevity escape velocity.*[4] We are escaping the limitations even of our lifespan, because when you tune into that God force in there as your Unique Self, as your Outrageous Lover Self, every cell in your body knows it. Every cell is turning on and saying *yes, I do believe.*

We celebrate that we are each an Outrageous Lover expressing unique acts of love. And we celebrate that we are able to express our unique acts of love together with everybody in this church, which itself is a glorious praise of God. Thank you. *Amen.*

EVOLUTIONARY LOVE CODE: EVOLUTION NEEDS MY OUTRAGEOUS ACTS OF LOVE

Let's talk about this idea that is very strong in Luria, the great mystic Luria, and which is also strong in Teilhard de Chardin. It is the deep truth within the thought that we are putting together.

> Your unique Outrageous Act of Love is happening in the Field of Evolution.

It is like in the Hasidic story about the man Yoselle, the holy miser, who in the sixteenth century is giving people ten kopeks and 15 kopeks under their doors, and we totally came together in this deep union on the essence of the story which is: *Whatever you are doing individually is participating in the larger Field of Evolution.*

I would like to share the download we received in the discovery process. Teilhard discovered the pattern of evolution and the direction of evolution toward greater consciousness, more freedom, and more loving order. The download is: **anything that you are doing in your life for greater consciousness, for more freedom, for more connectivity, for more love,**

---

4   Longevity escape velocity (LEV) is a hypothetical situation in which one's remaining life expectancy is extended longer than the time that is passing, leading to immortality.

for more Unique Self—you have the whole force of creation in there. You are doing that not as a single individual but:

You are an expression of the divine intent of the whole Universe.

We are all **coming from the same source with the same passion,** and in that sense, we are all created equal.

This is beautiful. That is so gorgeous. There is so much spirit in that. That is what carries us, even with all our imperfections.

We just solve it together transparently. This is part of what is at the core. **There are no words that can't be spoken.** We are delighted that everything can be spoken, everything can be worked out, everything is workable. And when it is workable, then there is no hidden story.

We want the inside and the outside to be the same.

- ◆ The way we talk to each other privately and publicly— the same.
- ◆ Outrageous Love all the way up and all the way down— the same.
- ◆ No words that can't be spoken—the same.

Do we ever disagree? For sure! Have we ever not been able to work through any issue with total love and delight? No, we always work everything through with love and delight. Because we honor each other so much.

The same love that you see between us *in public* is the same love we have *in private.* We are not killing each other in private. We are loving each other in private. We die to love each other. And we die to love our whole community and anyone who is involved in any of our projects and institutions. **The quality of our community is Outrageous Love.** It is not saccharine, it is not surface, it is a deep sense of commitment and integrity. No words that can't be spoken, and everything gets worked out at a higher level of consciousness.

I want to speak into that beautiful and gorgeous resonance, and I want to talk into this field that Teilhard de Chardin set up and that Luria set up, which is that **evolution is waiting for me.**

Evolution needs my Outrageous Acts of Love.

The world is not complete without me. That is true. These are our codes:

A separate self is a puzzle piece who is just walking along, it is a little wobbly, because the separate self isn't connected to the whole puzzle. And the separate self thinks he/she lives alone.

A True Self understands: *I am the Field. I am one. I am.* Either *I am the evolutionary Field,* or, as in Eastern mysticism, *I am.* A True Self is just one. That doesn't work either, because in the True Self there is no puzzle piece at all, there is just one monochromatic puzzle.

Unique Self: *I am a puzzle piece that completes the puzzle.* I am a puzzle piece that completes the puzzle.

Evolutionary Unique Self: that's what we are talking about here; the new human is an Evolutionary Unique Self. We awaken the species when, oh my God, when every human being realizes that *I am an Evolutionary Unique Self,* meaning: *I do not just complete the puzzle, I evolve the puzzle.* Because my unique *me-ness* is in the world, the world is more.

That is not narcissism. Narcissism is when I act out of my ego because I don't really get the realization: *the world is more, because there is me-ness in the world,* and that me giving my gift *evolves* the whole story.

The Evolutionary Unique Self says: *My Outrageous Acts of Love don't just complete the puzzle piece, they make the puzzle piece more radiant, more luminous, more stunning, more gorgeous, more beautiful. Oh my god.*

MY OUTRAGEOUS ACTS OF LOVE ARE MINE ALONE TO COMMIT

Friends, can I tell you a little story? Can I tell you the most beautiful little story in the world? It is such a great story; it is a story that comes from the deep mystical tradition, and it is a story that is in Teilhard de Chardin's field. I want to share it with you, beloveds, and just feel it with you. As I tell the story, I just want to invite you as you feel it, just to write down: *I am Evolutionary Love,* or *I have Outrageous Acts of Love to commit.* That is what we are implying: *I am Evolutionary Love.* That is our field. Our field is, *I am Evolutionary Love, I have Outrageous Acts of Love to commit, I am Evolutionary Love.*

Let me tell you the story. We need to realize that the story lives in that field and this story lives in that tone.

HASIDIC STORY OF YANKELE

The story is about a man. It takes place in the nineteenth century, and I have a Hebrew mystical image, so my stories often are Hasidic stories that take place in the mid-nineteenth century. Our story is about a man, and the name of the men in these stories is always Yankele. I don't know why. It is always Yankele.

> Yankele lives in this hamlet, and he hears that there is this little home available for sale. He saves all his money to go and buy this home because he is a little bit of a real estate guy. He realizes, *I can turn it around, and I can finally have enough money to feed my family for the rest of my life.* So, he borrows money from all of his friends, and he is going to buy this little house at the other

end of the *shtetl*. Think *Fiddler on the Roof* mid-19th century Poland. On the way he sees this wagon.

And this is one of our core stories. We want to try and download these stories into our source code, so they become our stories.

> He sees these two children tied to a wagon, and the wagon is going to the market. The two children are crying, just crying their heads off. And Yankele says to the man driving the wagon: *What are you doing?* He says, *I am going to sell these children. Why? Well, because you know the law. Their father couldn't pay his debt, the debt for three years he has owed my master, the count. He can't pay. We are taking his children, and we are selling them into the Russian army.*

When you get sold into the czar's army, this means you never come back.

> So, Yankele says: *What do you mean? I don't understand. How much money does he owe?* The driver barks: *He owes ten thousand rubles. Get away from here, gee (meaning Jew), get away from here. You would never have that much money.* Ten thousand rubles was an enormous amount of money. But Yankele had just collected exactly that amount of money. He had borrowed it from all his friends.

> So, without thinking, what does he do? He goes and he gives all ten thousand rubles to the wagon driver. He frees the children. The children were ecstatically delighted. He brings them back home. He is deeply in the moment. He is so in the moment. He brings them home. He brings them to the parents. The parents are ecstatic. He leaves the house and says: *Oh my God, what did I do? I just borrowed ten thousand rubles from all my friends and family. I have four children. I am never going to be able to pay it back. Within a few months they are going to come and take my children. What do I do?*

So, in Eastern Europe, in a Hasidic story, when you are not sure what to do, you go to the *beit midrash*, you go to the study hall.

30

He goes to the study hall, and he opens a page of the Talmud to try and lose himself in study because there is no prozac, no drugs, no ecstasy. He is going to lose himself in study. So, he is losing himself in study. There he is. He is losing himself in study.

Remember our field is: *I am Evolutionary Love. I have Outrageous Acts of Love to commit.*

I am speaking into *that* Evolutionary Field. De Chardin is with us, holding the space.

So, he is in the study hall, Yankele, and he is studying. Then this strange man walks in, with this great black outfit, very elegantly dressed who looks at him and says, *you seem very troubled? Could you tell me what is happening? Maybe I can help you?* You know, when you are sitting next to someone on the plane, the whole story spills out. The whole story. And the man says: *No problem!*

I have told the story before, but now I want to locate it in the field, so this becomes our story. This is not wisdo-tainment. We are laying down a field!

So the man says to him: *Wow, you did that beautiful thing! That was a mitzvah!*

In Hebrew wisdom, it is called a *mitzvah,* and a *mitzvah* means a commandment, but it also means *tzavta.* It means outrageous intimacy. You were outrageously intimate with Reality. I mean, what did Yankele do? He committed an Outrageous Act of Love, obviously! He didn't think. He just said to himself, *oh my god, these two children need to be freed right now. I have ten thousand rubles! Take it and you free the children.* That is an Outrageous Act of Love! But now his whole world could fall apart. He is not sure what to do. But this was his unique risk, but can he bear the risk?

So, the man says to him: *Don't worry, if you just give me the reward in heaven for your Outrageous Act of Love, I will give you the ten thousand rubles back.* And what did Yankele say? He said, *I can't!* The man says, *what do you mean? I mean, it will solve everything!*

Yankele is like: *I can't give you, I can't sell my Outrageous Act of Love to you. It's like—it was mine to do. I can't sell you the reward. It's not that I want the reward, but it just wouldn't honor what I did. That's who I am, that's my karma, that's my dharma.* And the man says: *You know what? I get it. I get it. You know what? I will give you ten thousand rubles, just sell me half of the reward for your Outrageous Act of Love.*

Yankele doesn't even think about it, he says: *I just can't do it!* The man again, *Well, how about a quarter? I will give you ten thousand rubles for a quarter.* And the man says to him: *I'll just give you ten thousand rubles, just give me a quarter of the reward for your Outrageous Act of Love.* And we know what Yankele said. He said: *No way, I can't!* And the man said: *You know what? That's so beautiful, that you refused to sell your Outrageous Act of Love. I am Elijah the prophet.*

Elijah in Hebrew mysticism is like the *bodhisattva*, the angel *bodhisattva*.

And Elijah says: *Because you refused to sell the reward for your Outrageous Act of Love and you lived in your unique risk, all opportunity and all prosperity and all blessing will open for you in the next months.* And so it was. Everything opened for Yankele. And his fortunes turned and new possibilities arose. He went on to have the most gorgeous and stunning life beyond what he ever imagined was possible.

Now, friends, hear this deeply. If this story was just a story about a great beautiful deed, it would not be an evolutionary story. It only becomes an evolutionary story when the man realizes: *I'm doing this for the sake of evolution itself. Evolution is living through me in this moment.* Our Outrageous Acts of Love tie beautifully into the evolutionary field as a whole. I am doing this for the sake of evolution. So, here is the last sentence: **I am doing this for the sake of evolution.** Oh my god! Just those words. Our words now are for the sake of evolution. That is where we are landing our Reality: for the sake of evolution. Yes, I am doing this for the sake of evolution. I am doing this for the sake of evolution! It is not just: I am Evolutionary Love. It is:

I am committing my Outrageous Act
of Love for the sake of evolution.

We are bringing this down, we are bringing the new species down! I could cry! The new humanity realizes that evolution stalls if I don't do my Outrageous Act of Love. I mean, I am going to have tears running down my cheeks. Can you imagine a world in which every person realizes: *I am committing my Outrageous Acts of Love for the sake of evolution?* Oh my God! And then our impulses of evolution come together, and together we can do something that we could not do separately. We can make our contribution together. We are praying together: *I want to know what love is.* And we know it is Evolutionary Love. We are going to change by growing this collective. **I am evolution, I am doing this for the sake of evolution.**

WE HAVE A DREAM, AND THE DREAM HAS US!

When you say *Yes* to the evolutionary impulse within you, that *Yes* is your pay. You get so paid up by the joy of that evolutionary impulse infusing you with its passion, its genius, its love. Instead of just being a simple person trying to get something done, you are already given the joy of the expression of the Divine uniquely as you. That is a huge reward for anybody who says *Yes* to this. Our contribution is to that *Yes* inside us and inside everybody else. Let's think of a planet filled with this joy and with this creativity that is the unique gift of each person coming alive and imagine this gift going also to where it fits best in the planetary awakening. If you are in health or in education or economics, you will be able to give it your all. Any contribution is a contribution to the fulfillment of the Evolutionary Lover in you, to the Evolutionary Lover worldwide, and the planetary awakening in love. I keep thinking of the Martin Luther King speech, "I have a dream." I have a dream that we will be a participant in the creation of that Evolutionary Love affair on a planetary scale, and if any group would be guided to that it would be us.

Oh my God, I have a dream! I have a dream that we participate and catalyze the new human. It's the new humanity, and we can go all the way together. I have a dream!

Let's do this together as we join the collective: We have a dream! We have a dream. We are in that moment when we move from "I have a dream" to "we have a dream". We have a dream!

We sing together *I want to know what love is* because we don't skip our personal, broken lives, or our personal whole lives. **It's the poignancy of our personal lives that we pour into the passion of the evolution.** We have a dream. And the dream has us.

The dream that we are dreaming is the impulse of creation in every one of us, and our *Yes* turns the dream into Reality.

CHAPTER THREE

A NEW VISION OF IDENTITY: THE NEW HUMAN

Episode 53 — October 28, 2017

THE EVOLUTIONARY IMPULSE MOVES INTIMATELY AND AUTHORITATIVELY

Evolutionary Love is the inner core of Reality. Tune in, feel what that inner core feels like. Recognize it. It is Evolutionary Love, the love of Creation, the love of God. **The quality of Evolutionary Love is intimacy, which is the feeling of your internal reality being Outrageous Love.** That love is an expression of intimacy. So you and that impulse of creation are one. They are one uniquely—as you!

Let's tune in to that inner Reality of our being. Feel it. The inner of the inner is the Creator alive as you. The tension creates this Reality. Attend to and put your attention on the inner Creator alive *uniquely* as you.

Each one of these codes is not a noun, but it is a verb: unfolding, emerging, new, now.

In other words, the billions of years of evolutionary impulse, which is Outrageous Love, is coded as your intimate expression of creativity in love. When you express it, you are tuned into the *entire story* of creation

as you. You are not just walking around as a separate person. You are walking around as an expression of God.

And every moment—in a way, if you take snapshots of yourself—is a snapshot of that expression coming through you, *unfolding* as you, *vibrating* as you, *feeling* as you.

Let's do this together, let's create the shared frequency of each person in a chorus of divine love, by experiencing *directly and intimately* the impulse of evolution as it is expressing in our unique love, as it is the expression of God *uniquely as us.*

One small group doing that *now* changes the world. Let's stay experiencing that inner impulse as the Divine—*intimately and authoritatively*—you and me, each one of us. We take this intimacy and beauty of the internal experience of God into our hands.

ECSTASY MEANS TO BE BESIDE THE OLD VISION OF SELF

We are in Florence in the beginning of the Renaissance.

We are in Bethlehem in the advent moment of Christianity.

We are in the desert Sinai with Moses or the Desert Fathers.

We are with Confucius,

We are with Lao Tzu.

We are convening the new vision.
We are convening the new vision of
identity, the new vision of community,
the new Universe Story.

Da Vinci with his friends in Florence could not address the plague and the Black Death, and he had no answers for the war and the destruction of the premodern period—they were merely trying to work out some economic social solution to the problem. What da Vinci and his colleagues needed to do was **to raise all boats by articulating this new vision of identity, community, Universe Story, practice, a new map**—the five great keys.

It is only that new story that changes everything.

We are here at this moment in time after the deconstructions of postmodernity. We are ready to articulate the new vision. This new vision is no less dramatic, it is no less stunning, even more so, because it is evolving. It takes into account the best of what came before. It is as much a paradigm shift as in the Renaissance; not some clever New Age paradigm shift, but rooted deeply in the best of the interior and exterior sciences. It is the best vision of Reality that is so dramatically new and yet transcends and includes everything. It is the only response we have today, and it is our great responsibility, our ability-to-respond to the existential risk, that threatens the very existence of our planet.

And we are ecstatic, meaning we are beside ourselves! To be beside ourselves is to be beside the old vision of self.

Like Rumi says, *Let me take you out of yourself and lift you like a prayer to the sky.*

The only way we can lift like a prayer to the sky is to take ourselves out of ourselves, meaning out of the old vision of self, out of the contracted vision of self and to articulate a new vision of the new human and the new humanity, to awaken this new humanity, and to awaken this new Universe Story. That is what we are here to do. We are here to love each other madly and to participate directly in the evolution of love. We are here to participate directly by *being together* the new human. And *becoming together* the new humanity. It *is it*, it is not *about it*.

We are articulating together a new set of what we call Evolutionary Love Codes. Our code that we are working with is:

Reality is not a fact; it is a story. It is an Outrageous Love Story.

As Solomon wrote: *Its insides are lined with love.* But lined with Outrageous Love! It is not ordinary love, it is an Evolutionary Love. And Evolutionary Love means—and this is the essence of our code—that **we live in an Intimate Universe.**

There are several Tenets of Intimacy, and the first tenet is: **We live in an Intimate Universe.** Oh my God, wow! And in an Intimate Universe, Infinity discloses its intimacy. The god you don't believe in doesn't exist. **God is not merely infinity or even infinite power.**

God is the Infinity of Intimacy.

When any two of us have a personal moment, it is not just our small separate selves getting personal. It is not just someone getting personal, it is an expression of the larger, personal Fields of Reality itself.

Reality is personal.

The Buddhists got it half right when they said: *Move beyond personality, access the impersonal,* or *the process,* as the evolutionary people say (and that is us), but beyond the process *we are the inside of the process, we are the inside of the impersonal Field of Consciousness,* which is a higher level of personal.

Level one: personality, separate self, skin encapsulated ego. That is good because ego exists in the mind of God, and separation exists also in the mind of God.

Level two is either pure consciousness from an *advaita vedanta* Eastern mystical perspective or from a Western mystical perspective: Pure consciousness, essence, *I am*. Or from an evolutionary perspective it is *pure process*. The process is everything.

- Level one is personality.
- Level two is the process in the Field of Consciousness.
- Level three is the ultimate intimate personal— Evolutionary Lover.

We are all Evolutionary Lovers. We live in an Intimate Universe.

The Infinity of Intimacy that knows us and holds us. It is not just personal at the level of personality.

Intimacy is everything.
Intimacy is everywhere.

THE MYSTERY IS DESIGNED FOR EVOLUTIONARY LOVE

Feel the fierceness of this! The Infinite Intimacy and the story of it *as us*. Just take a brief moment and *re-member*. Let's take remembering literally, like: our origin of creation, mystery beyond mystery, totally designed for Evolutionary Love to become conscious.

If we want to go into the deepest intention of creation it would be exactly that intent that originated then gets to be recognized as your intent. And what does that intent hold in terms of Evolutionary Love? The entire genius of evolution is Evolutionary Love. And I love the idea of the first quarks.

There is something so touching about it. After the Big Bang come these entities called quarks and are attracted to each other. I identified with the quarks. I am a little quark and I have no idea what I am doing because I have just come through the Big Bang, which itself I didn't understand at all. And here I am, attracted to another quark. Just think of the compelling

Evolutionary Love that is going on right there, because as those quarks get attracted, they create.

They really create atoms, molecules, and eventually cells. And I am a quark, I am attracted. When I say *Yes* to that attraction, look what happened! You take the journey of the Evolutionary Love up from the single cells and just put your attention on every cell in your body—it is all an expression of the intimacy of love of those first cells.

It could have been enough just to be a cell, but what happened is that there was an attraction for other cells. Just imagine the awesome journey of the attraction, cell to cell, the evolution from single cells to multicellular animals. Not only are they attracted to each other, they are coordinated into whole bodies. The cells joining to form multicellular animals are an *awesome intelligence*. Not only are those cells attracted—this is going to be showing what it means for us—but **when the cells join they become more of who they are. They become more of their uniqueness and they become enormously creative.**

This would be just thinking of single-celled animals, but then take them all up to the earliest, earliest humans. Well, of course, at the same time there has to be an entire Earth. And it has to have all the plants and all the grass, and all the vegetables, and all the nourishment, and all the animals being created by this Evolutionary Love.

Let's take an awesome moment and consider that the Evolutionary Love in all of that is intimately in us alive as an intimate, Unique-Self expression of *this,* following the vast story of evolution, as Evolutionary Lovers, aware that our internal impulse is *that,* and that we are attracted to each other.

If our joining of our genius with each other is anything like what happened to the quarks and the single cells and the multi-cells, just think of what this means for this vast planetary organism! How each of us is uniquely called to emerge from this point where it could go into devolution and self-destruction or into evolution and the creation of the new. Realize, you are a cell attracted into joining with each other to realize the evolutionary impulse for a greater whole.

Tune in to the *that*, what it feels like when we are attracted to each other and join and unite. We are part of this awesome mystery of *that*, starting with the quarks and right up to us now. *That* which began with this joining as a quark, as single cells, as multi-cells, as animals and humans, and now as *evolutionary humans* joining genius in intimate expression of the Divine.

Let's feel inside ourselves the enormity of emerging love—God's love.

And feel it as an invisible impulse of creation **with all the genius inherent in it from everything that came before it in every cell**—the eye, the ear, the thumb, oh my God.

Let's tune in together into the genius joining of Evolutionary Lovers creating—creating what?

Is it as radically new as a person? Is it as radically new as a planet?

What is that newness that the intimacy is now creating?

We have said that the purpose is a **planetary awakening in love through a Unique Self Symphony, joining by the very same tendency that got everything else to join**.

Joining!

On the one hand, we are fearing the destruction of our life-support system, and on the other hand—everywhere where universal evolutionary human beings occur—are we not only expecting, but *intending and experiencing* in the quantum field, in the zero-point energy, the instantaneous manifestation and connectivity of the next level of intimacy on a social scale. Where—whoever with and wherever we are feeling this intimacy—

we are then becoming more of the frequency of the Divine together. We are sharing the innovations and the creative solutions in a transforming world.

Is it not awesome that it creates *this*?!

ALLUREMENT ALL THE WAY UP THE EVOLUTIONARY CHAIN

Oh my God, I mean it is true. It does not get more awesome. When we *get* that we live in an Intimate Universe and that I *am* a quark, I *am* Evolutionary Love like the quark is Evolutionary Love, I realize that we liberate love. **Here is the key to the Intimate Universe**—picking up the thread as we weave words in one voice, and we join not genes but the higher genes of the individual genius of Unique Self, and we come together in this WeSpace—here is the gorgeous thing: What we realize in this Evolutionary Code, when we say: *Its insides are lined with love.*

I wrote an essay called "Evolutionary Love," and it starts with quarks and the feminine co-Creator—let's make it personal—She says, *I am a quark. Let's not talk about quarks, let's be a quark*, okay? So, I am a quark!

I just want to invite everyone for a second just to write this: *I am a quark.* Now, I am more than a quark, okay? I am more than a quark but I am not less than a quark. Does everyone get that? I am a quark. I am a little quarky. I am a quark. I am a quark! First you have to be a quark before we transcend and include a quark—just be a quark! I am a quark. Don't be smart, don't be clever, just be a quark! I am a dancing quark! Just be quarky with me! Let's just be a little quarky in church! But actually this is not just cute, it is a shift in identity! Anybody not quarking here? We have to quark into this! I am a quark! I know you are. I am a joyful quark. Quark here, quark there, quark everywhere. Oh there is also a lepton, alright, we have a couple of leptons, too. Fine!

I need to *get* that I am a quark, that I am more than a quark, and I am not less than a quark. And you know what a quark feels? What the quark!

What does a quark feel, friends? A quark feels that, oh my God, *I am allured.*

And at the moment of the Big Bang, the great flying forth, the quarks only survive if three quarks come together—the original *ménage à trois.* At the beginning of Reality there is this Holy Trinity.

And a quark can't live by itself because a quark is allured to other quarks, but not just any other quarks. Quarks are allured to specific other quarks to dance with, and then they form stable depth-relationships with other quarks. And no quark can live alone. It is not good for a quark to be alone. We have scripture on this.[5] Oh my God!

And then quarks come together and they form something new through the configurations of their intimacy. And what they form new is called an atom.

EVOLUTION OF INTIMACY

An atom! Are you willing to play with me all the way? Here we go. Ready? I am an atom. Anyone willing to do it with me? I am an atom. Any atoms? Give me some atoms here. Do we have any atoms here? I am an atom. Don't stop with being a quark, okay? That is a regression. People are thinking, *oh, I am just going to be a little quark. I am not going to be an atom. No, I am just to be a quark. Really? Not me. I am not going to write that down.*

Give me some atoms. I am an atom. The atoms come together. We are moving fast now, okay? Let me *atom* and say: *I am a molecule.* Any molecules? I am a molecule. We are now moving up the evolutionary chain. And molecules are allured to each other. And I am a complex molecule, a complex molecule. And now I am waking up as a cell. I am a cell. And these cells are allured to each other. And they form—ready? I am a multi-cell! I am a multi-something, like a multivitamin. And I am a multi-cell. And **what is driving this entire process is allurement.** And now I am an organism. I am an organism! And now I am a complex organism.

5 Genesis 2:18: "It's not good for man to be alone."

And, ready for this? We are about to take a leap and a jump here. I am a plant! I am a plant. I did a leap and I am a plant. I'm an organism, a plant, and now, as allurement happens—ready? I am fish in the sea. I am fish in the sea. And we know that, friends, we know the processes that happen in plants. We breathe in and out with plants. The structure of genetics and fish live in us, and I am an early animal! I'm an early animal and I am a mammal. And I am a later mammal. And I am a hominid walking on the savanna a million years ago.

What is driving this entire process is Evolutionary Love.

The Universe is not random, is not by chance.

There's a random and chance dimension in how some of the mutations happen, but it happens in the larger context of Evolutionary Love. The Universe is guided by Evolutionary Love Codes that are the principles of an Intimate Universe. **That Intimate Universe is yearning to awaken as a new species. The Intimate Universe is yearning to become a new human.**

I am an early prehistoric hunter-gatherer. That is me. I am an early prehistoric hunter-gatherer. And I am thinking about my expanse of time as fifteen minutes, and I escape the bison that wants to kill me and my wife. And then, oh my God, we're allured and I take care of my wife, and I take care of my daughter. And I realize that I don't sexualize my daughter, which is the beginning of the family. I protect my daughter, which is a new expression of Evolutionary Love that never existed before.

And then we come together and let's farm a little bit! Hey, honey, you want to start a farm? Let's start a farm! And I'm doing agrarian now, and there are early tools, horticulture, and later tools. And then I come together in larger and larger units of interaction and love. My love expands. I don't just love my clan, I love my entire tribe. And my love expands. I don't just love my tribe, I love the entire kingdom. I am allured to everybody in the kingdom.

And then my love expands, oh my God, and then we go through these thousands of years, and finally I burst forth with da Vinci in the Renaissance, and I realize, *I don't just love Florence.* Although da Vinci battles Florence his whole life, he gets to this moment where he says, *I love all the Italian city-states.*

And then I burst forward, and I'm going to finally get into the French Enlightenment, when the guillotine stops with some aggressive movement. I realized, oh my God, I love all of humanity. I have moved from **ethnocentric** to **worldcentric** love.

And intimacy is expanding. I love all of humanity, but I'm still into hot dogs and hamburgers because I don't think a lot about cows.

And then I break even beyond that when I become **cosmocentric**. And I am intimate with all of Reality. I am Evolutionary Man and Evolutionary Woman.

I am evolution. Evolution has always been conscious, but now evolution is conscious *in me*. **I am conscious of evolution.**

I realize that who I am is:

I am evolution. I am Evolutionary Love.

And friends, are we ready to write: *I am...* I know this is a big phrase, but ready? *I am a unique expression of Evolutionary Love.* I know, that is a lot of writing. How about this? *I am Evolutionary Love unique.* I am Evolutionary Love unique. I am Evolutionary Love unique, that is who I am. I am a unique expression of Evolutionary Love.

Oh my God, I am a unique expression of Evolutionary Love. And the quarks and the atoms and the molecules and the cells and everything, all lives in me. And intimacy has driven Reality to create new and higher and deeper configurations of intimacy, and we are reclaiming an identity.

I want to bring you this: *I am a unique expression of Evolutionary Love.* Write it, cry it out, shout it out, so we can evolve love together! I want to bring you here. *Let us get how real this is.* **I am a unique expression of Evolutionary Love!** Let's bring this into the *New York Times!*

REALIZE OUR DEEPER IDENTITY: THE NEW HUMAN

Our friend David Brooks wrote a column about what was happening in St. Petersburg a hundred years ago. In the column he is citing a guy named John Reed, who was in St. Petersburg a hundred years ago watching Lenin and Trotsky and the rest of the Bolsheviks take over Russia. **Why did they win?** Why did they win against the Democrats who wanted Russia to move in a much more sweet and liberal direction? Because he says, *The thing you notice is that the Communists had religion. They had secular religion. They believed in something. They had a clear intellectual framework that explained events.* The problem with their intellectual framework was that it was dogmatic. It was based in only one dimension of Reality, which is all about economics and about means of production. It was a weak explanation. But they had a sense of identity, while the Russian Democrats had lost moral authority.

- ◆ They didn't have the trust of the people.
- ◆ They didn't trust themselves because they stopped believing in anything.

And he describes the first ten days of Lenin. And then David Brooke starts talking about the ten days of Trump and **why Trump is sweeping parts of America. Why did he get elected?** Why did he defeat the entire Obama-Clinton machine, the most powerful democratic machine in history? Why did he defeat a field of 17 mega-wealthy republican candidates, including the entire Bush machine? What did he do?

It is really easy to deride the guy. And he deserves a little derision because he is doing some crazy stuff. And he is not behaving very presidentially. He is not inspiring moral leadership. But if we just demonize him, we are going to miss the point. In other words, what is Trump about? I want you to really get this deeply: **Trump is speaking into a context in which there is a complete loss of identity.** What Americans are doing is that they're struggling for identity, asking, *Who am I?* Trump doesn't have a positive new vision of identity, but here is the story: neither did Clinton!

The liberal world has not articulated a new answer to the question of *Who am I?* There is no positive vision of identity. We don't know who we are.

All the liberal world can tell us is:

- I'm a skin-encapsulated ego. I am a separate self.
- And I am a victim, I have to make sure not to be a victim.
- I have to protect my separate selfhood, which is momentous.

That is a momentous advance! We have to stand firm against any form of sexual harassment. And any form of victimization. That is the great accomplishment of the postmodern separate self. Don't get into my space, get out of my face. You have no right to touch me. I am protected.

That is beautiful. That is holy. That is gorgeous.

But it is not enough. I need to have a positive, noble vision of identity, I need to realize, I am not just a separate self, who is a dangling modifier in the vocabulary of the cosmic scroll.

I need to realize a deeper identity: I am a new human!

And a new human realizes:

I am a quark! I am an atom! I am a molecule! I am a salad! It all lives in me! And evolution is awakening in me, as me, and through me. I am a new configuration of intimacy driven by Evolutionary Love. I am an Evolutionary Lover. I am Evolutionary Love uniquely expressed. I have Outrageous Acts of Love to commit that can be done by no one that ever was, is, or will be. I am a unique expression. I am, and that is our code:

I am God's unique intimacy.

I live in an Intimate Universe, and I am God's unique intimacy. I am an Evolutionary Unique Self. And together as Evolutionary Unique Selves we form a *Homo universalis*.

We come together as a new species, as a new human. I am Evolutionary Love uniquely expressed, and Reality needs my service—as our previous codes say. Reality needs my gift.

TRANSCENDING PREMODERNITY, MODERNITY, AND POSTMODERNITY

I want to tell something to David Brooks from *The New York Times*. I mean David, my dear friend, you don't get it. David quotes Jonathan Sacks, who is a colleague of mine, who is a wonderful Orthodox Rabbi. And Jonathan says: *America was based on biblical categories and it was about marriages, families, and congregations.* And Sacks says: *Today we have lost our biblical categories of strong marriages and families, and communities.* And David Brooks ends his piece saying: *We need this new vision of identity.* And he says: *Frankly, I think America's traditional biblical ethic is still lurking somewhere in the national DNA, but there has to be a leader who can restore it to life.*

No, David, no! You missed the point! **Yes, we are going to *transcend and include* biblical ethic.** For sure. **The biblical ethic that understood the Infinity of Intimacy, yes! But the biblical ethic that was ethnocentric**

and homophobic, no! And the old vision of marriage isn't going to carry us the same way. We need the old vision of marriage, and the best of it, and new visions of relationship. We live in a world in which more than 50% of America is not in a traditional marriage.

That is not what it is about, my friends. It is not about the old biblical epic. You get it? We have to take and transcend and include. **The old biblical ethic was premodern. It was ethnocentric and homophobic**.

- ◆ We have to take the best of the old biblical ethic, not the worst, and evolve it.
- ◆ We have to take the best of modernity and evolve it.
- ◆ We have to take the best of postmodernity and evolve it.

Why did Trump get elected? Because we didn't articulate a new vision. Evolution stalled, as my friend Ken Wilber likes to say. **Evolution's stalled because postmodernity deconstructed all of modernity and premodernity, but didn't offer a new vision of identity.**

We are about offering that new vision of identity.

- ◆ Who am I?

I am Evolutionary Love uniquely expressed. I am an Evolutionary Unique Self.

- ◆ Who are we?

We are the new humanity. We are the Unique Self Symphony. Each of us committing our Outrageous Acts of Love. Coming together in this new vision.

It is the Evolutionary Love practices and the Evolutionary Love Codes that take us the next step, that take us into community which is Unique Self Symphony.

When David Brooks ends his column by saying: *Let's find the biblical ethic,* he misses the point.

Here is the last piece. What Trump has done is, my friends: he has taken the shadow of premodernity, the shadow of modernity and the shadow of postmodernity and tried to put them together.

His shadow of premodernity is—he says, *I am supported by the fundamentalist world.* Blessing to our fundamentalist friends, who get a lot right, but they got a lot wrong. Trump says, I got supported by fundamentalists, I have Mike Pence who wants to hang the homosexuals. Really? That is the **shadow of premodernity**.

Then Trump is the **shadow of modernity**. Modernity is business. And Trump says on national television in a debate: *I don't pay contractors who did work for me, because I am a good businessman.* That is the shadow of capitalism. That is the tragedy. It is crony capitalism, it is the shadow of modernity. Was there any big fundamentalism, crony capitalism, bad business?

And then we know that Trump is the **shadow of postmodernity**. Because postmodernity is about post-truth. And Trump takes post-truth out of the academy and he makes post-truth—facts don't matter, truth doesn't matter—into an actual instrument of policy.

Trump weaves together the three shadows of premodernity and modernity and postmodernity into a new tragic identity.

My problem with Trump is not his policies. There are good Republican think tanks. There are good Democratic think tanks. My trouble with Trump is—he is not a new *Homo religiosus.*

We need a new human and a new humanity. We need to know, *I am Evolutionary Love.* I am a unique expression of Evolutionary Love. And we are Evolutionary Unique Selves who come together as *Homo universalis.* We can look at each other's eyes, my friends. We can respond to what David Brooks doesn't yet understand. We can share this vision, because it is only this new vision, this evolution of love that can respond to the second shock of existence.

WE ARE AT THE POINT OF EVOLUTION OR DEVOLUTION

We think we are going to make it through. Evolutionary Love is an expression of the consciousness of evolution that created everything.

Conscious evolution is evolution that became conscious as Evolutionary Love. Wow! It not only became conscious as Evolutionary Love. We ask, *how does Evolutionary Love work?*

How do quarks get together and create all this?

> *What we are learning through our science and our technology and our intuition is: that we're carrying the story about how to make it work.*

To be very pragmatic, it's not going to work without that. We are at the point of the big devolution of our planet, at the crossroads between evolution or devolution.

Contribute to the evolution of Evolutionary Love.

Let's assemble the community, the co-creators, the evolutionary beings that love and are intelligent enough to heal the Earth, free the people, explore the universe.

Let's create evolutionary community planet-wide and give your contribution to evolving the world!

How could anyone ever tell you[6] that you are anything less than beautiful, how could anyone ever tell you that you are less than whole? How could anyone fail to notice that our love is just a miracle and how deeply we are connected in our souls.

What a delight to be alive, friends! This is it!

---

6   "How Could Anyone," song by Libby Roderick.

CHAPTER FOUR

REVOLUTION THROUGH LOVE AND EVOLUTION OF TECHNOLOGIES

Episode 54 — November 3, 2017

LOVE IS A UNIQUE SELF PERCEPTION

Begin with the realization that our Unique Self perception is love.

Resonate with that uniqueness *within us, as us, as love.*

But as Evolutionary Love, Outrageous Love, as the love that creates the entire Universe as self.

The greatest possible vision of self is to awaken as universal love, Evolutionary Love, creative love, Outrageous Love—*as you*!

In that sense you are resonating with the whole universal process *as you*. Self-perception means we are perceiving a love that has never been seen before in human history.

We didn't really know much about the Evolutionary Story of creation until recently.

EVOLUTIONARY LOVE CODE: UNIQUE SELF PERCEPTION

Love is a Unique Self perception. Self-love is a perception of one's own Unique Self.

As we resonate this Evolutionary Love code, experience everybody's self, resonating together, feeling the impulse of evolution within us in a field of awesome awakening.

We are unfolding a series of Evolutionary Love Codes. Everything is related to that. For example, when we look at something like sexual harassment, what it means is, *I don't see you.*

- If I see you, I say, oh my God! God is in you!
- If I see you, I see the divine spark in you.
- If I see you, I see your infinite Unique Self.

Love is a unique perception.

We feel together that love is a Unique Self perception. We want to bring this vision of love, not to one or two or three or four, but to tens and hundreds of millions of people around the world.

I, Marc, was sitting with the Dalai Lama, in his room in Dharamsala. When I said to him, *love is a Unique Self perception,* he jumped off his seat and said, *Beautiful! Beautiful! Beautiful!* (He does that! He is so excited.)

Now, why is it so exciting? Why is it such a big deal? Why did the Dalai Lama jump out of his seat and say, *Beautiful! Beautiful!?*

To say it simply, we have made love small.

We have made love so small.

We have taken love, which is so huge, and we have made it into this little *Harlequin* romance moment.

What is the universe? What is our basic credo? What is the new Universe Story rooted in the best reading of evolutionary science? A new Universe

Story that is rooted in chaos theory, complexity theory, all the interior sciences of the great traditions, and in everything we know of our lives. When we put it all together, what do we know?

- We know Reality is not a fact, it is a story.
- It is not an ordinary story, it is a love story.
- It is not a harlequin romance, it is not an ordinary love story, it is an Outrageous Love Story.
- Reality is an Evolutionary Love story.

Reality is moving to higher and higher, deeper and deeper levels of care, concern, and love. In that process of evolution, we recognize that it is not a static love story, but it is an Evolutionary Love Story.

Evolutionary Love *drives* the whole story. It drives quarks to become molecules and molecules to become atoms.

But not only is it an Evolutionary Love Story, **love itself evolves in the love story! It is the story of the evolution of love!**

Wow!

In the beginning, we just love our own little survival clan: **egocentric love.**

But then we love our whole country, even the people we don't need for survival! That is a bigger love, that is **sociocentric or ethnocentric love.**

But then we get to this place in history, to something that began to appear around the Renaissance, where we actually love the whole world—**worldcentric love.** And finally:

We are in love with all of Reality, and all of Reality loves as me, that is what we call cosmocentric love. This is the evolution of love.

How does the evolution of love happen in this very moment? Love evolution awakens *as me*. I am evolution's eyes. I am the eyes of the evolutionary impulse itself. To really get our code is to know:

To be a lover is to see with God's eyes.

To be a lover is to see with evolution's eyes, and when I see you with evolution's eyes.

I know that:

- There's nothing accidental in your story.
- Every detour is a destination.
- Your/my holy and broken *Hallelujahs* are all part of this larger tapestry of life.

This is an invitation for my healing and transformation, so that we can be a lover seeing with God's eyes.

I can be a lover giving my unique gifts. I can be in service and contribution—in delight, in Eros—as the very eyes, ears, face, hands, body, embodiment of evolution itself.

That is why the Dalai Lama jumped out of his seat.

We have made love small. We have taken love away from being the fabric of the Cosmos, although both interior and exterior sciences reveal to us that love is the very fabric of All-That-Is.

We have exiled love in three ways:

- Exile one: We have made love only human.
- Exile two: We have made love only a human emotion.
- Exile three: We have made love only a very *specific* emotion—infatuation. Love is to be infatuated for a few months, then I fall out of love.

We have taken *The Universe: A Love Story* and exiled it.

Love is a Unique Self perception. Reality is evolution becoming conscious. Conscious Evolution happens when I awaken as evolution's eyes, as an Evolutionary Lover.

The way we do it is by praying the *holy and the broken Hallelujah*. We bring everything before God and we say, *God, you see us. You see us so clearly.* We are Gods seeing each other. "God-ing." Therefore, we can ask for everything, because we know that *it's* all *part of the larger love story*.

My love story is part of the larger love story of Reality itself.

With the holy and broken *Hallelujah*, our hymn, **we pray** not to the *Santa Claus god* but **to the evolutionary God, to the Infinity of Intimacy that knows our name.** The personal God that lives in us and holds us, the God that Rumi talks about, when he says, *let's fall into the arms of the Beloved.* We are going to offer prayer, and the way we pray is that we ask for everything! Because that is what it means to be a lover who sees and who is seen with God's eyes. The holy and broken *Hallelujah*.

We pray to the evolutionary God, to the Infinity of Intimacy, that knows our name.

We evolve Reality together, and we evolve love. Do you remember *Avatar*, that James Cameron movie? When she says, *I see you?* Equally, we turn to each other and say, *I see you, I love you.*

VOCATIONAL AROUSAL AND JOINING GENIUS

I have been contemplating love internally *as myself.* I have been contemplating evolution internally as *evolution needing me.* Here's what I have noticed about the **inner love: it is all working by attraction.**

Inner love, with all its intimacy, is not a lonely path as we evolve.

No!

The Universe: A Love Story and conscious evolution say exactly this: quarks are attracted to quarks, electrons to electrons. Just think of the awesome love that brought single cells together with more single cells. Why did they join? Because they became more when they became multi-cellular.

That *becoming more* keeps happening all the way up to you and me and all of us.

That is the gorgeousness of what we can do now.

Is anybody going to become their full Unique Self all alone? Is anybody going to be able to be evolution in person, going out into a world that doesn't recognize evolution or personhood yet, all by themselves? Are we going to do this alone? No!

The answer is to fulfill the intimacy of self-evolution *within* us, we have to have community!

Jesus said, *where two or more are gathered in my name, there I am in their midst*. We can say, where two or more are gathered in the name of that Unique Self, which is the Divine Self—joined as Unique Self Symphony— there *we* are.

The "we" that we are becoming is actually *a new we*. The evolutionary impulse is becoming conscious as Outrageous Lovers in ourselves. To join at the time of this meta-crisis is existential necessity. Otherwise, we could go down towards devolution. The reason why the Evolutionary Church has come into existence at precisely the moment of a crossroads between devolution and evolution is that it is absolutely necessary. We have created a vehicle where, let's say 50 or more join with another 50 or more, and so on, until the Evolutionary Unique Self of each one of us is expanding into *becoming more* through Unique Self Symphony.

For the growing and deepening of the community **we need the gift of each one of us Outrageous Lovers**, to give our gift uniquely as ourselves, to give to each other and eventually to the larger world.

If I had to think of one thing that would make the greatest difference in shifting the larger world away from a devolution trajectory—which is based on separation, competition, and despair—towards evolution and joining together, we would do what nature does: **We would join genius.** I would like to declare that:

* Evolutionary Church is going to be a new vehicle for the joining of genius!

When we pray, let us pray to be able to give our gift the whole way. **Because the deep self in everyone is yearning to be expressed more fully.** None of us can do it alone and none of us can do it without a community of lovers! Let's declare in our collective prayer that by joining in community as Unique Selves, as a perception of love—just like nature has joined from single cell to multi-cell to animal to human—we are going to create the new human and the new humanity.

TO LOVE IS TO GIVE

We are not going to create the new human and the new humanity by just focusing on the greatness of prayer. We are inviting each other to form a community of Unique Selves for the sake of everyone giving their gift more fully into a world in existential crisis.

It could be the most important thing that is happening anywhere!

That might seem a bit of a *mad Outrageous Lover* speaking, but if you look at what is happening in the world and then look at this community you can see that this is a place where we are going to go the whole way. It is right here!

This could change the source code of all of Reality.

Here people are really going to be nurtured vocationally by attraction, to join genius, to give their gift of love through loving.

I would like to declare that *we are going to become an evolutionary community that has never existed before*, probably as unique as the very early church was, who believed in the *Second Coming of Christ*. We don't necessarily believe in the *Second Coming of Christ*, but we believe in the evolution of humanity toward a planetary awakening in love through Unique Self Symphonies.

I am now praying to give everything that I can to create the Evolutionary Church collective, which is the first collective on this Earth dedicated to self-evolution at this level, when the world is in crisis.

I am asking for the liberation of humanity *in you* as a lover.

I would like to just take a jump forward and imagine that we have already done this, that within six months, we have a next level of loving each other, of giving gifts, of expressing our unique gifts. That is my request. I am asking for liberation, for co-creation, and for more love through creating community together.

To be a lover is to be a giver. The word in Hebrew—it is beautiful—is *hav.* It means *to love, to be aflame, and to give.*

Can we take this church forward as they did before in Bethlehem and as da Vinci did with his cohorts in Florence?

Can we enact a revolution in evolution? It's always a new technology that does so—it's always the next step.

ENACTING REVOLUTION THROUGH NEW TECHNOLOGY

I will tell you something wild. These days we have the possibility of seeing each other on the screen. When we look at each other, I can see you, you can see me, we can see each other. How awesome is that?

Do you remember Franklin Delano Roosevelt? He runs for president. Why does he win? He is the first person who knows how to use radio!

Then JFK runs for president against Richard Nixon at a particular point, and he wins in 1960. Why does he win? Because he is the first person who knows how to use television!

And then Barack Obama runs for office, and why does he win? He is the first person who knows how to use email!

Shiva Ayyadurai, a young Indian man who is running for Senate, was the person who created email when he was a high school student. He created email in the Smithsonian, and Barack Obama wins the election because he creates this massive direct email campaign. That is number three.

Number four: Trump wins because he knows how to use Twitter.

So, we went:

- From a person who had to use radio (FDR),
- To a person who knew how to use television (JFK),
- To a person who knew how to use email (Obama),
- To a person who knew how to use Twitter, Facebook, and social media (Trump).

What do you see here? You see that the evolution of technology, which is an exterior, and our ability to deploy technology, directly affects interiors.

The Evolutionary Church, my friends, is the first online church committed to not one denomination, not an ethnocentric God that someone owns. It is not televangelism, it is "evoluti-angelism."

How would we call that? We will have to work on that word.

In other words, we are bringing *the good news,* but not for profit, and not for a Mercedes Benz (although someone did sing, *Oh Lord, won't you buy me a Mercedes Benz*[7]).

---

7   Janis Joplin, singer and songwriter, 1970.

---

*We are together enacting a
social revolution in which tens of
millions of people will be connected
worldwide as a Unique Self
Symphony, a community of lovers
seeing with God's eyes.*

We will be able to enact social change, and to enact healing, and to enact transformation, and to enact synergistic democracy, and to enact a politics of Evolutionary Love.

The way to do it is to have tens of millions of people, and then hundreds of millions of people connected to the Evolutionary Church. It is not going to be one church. It is not going to be everyone tuning into one or two leading figures. There are going to be dozens and hundreds of Evolutionary Churches in a network, in a node, around the world. We will see billions of people rising. But not rising merely to get on Facebook, so that my creativity is then used for profit by a small group of oligarchs who own Amazon and Facebook and Google. It is only about a hundred people who own Amazon, Google, Twitter, and who profit. It is oligarchy.

But that is not what we are talking about here. This is not an old capitalistic model; it is *genuine Facebook*. It is *Unique Self Facebook*.

Another element of our love affair is *vocational arousal*. One of our specialties is helping people find each other to co-create—**if you want to really express love in the world, you have to find partners.**

We are a community of people who want to give what somebody else uniquely needs.

If we imagine it, it will be.

The word *Adam,* in the original Hebrew, means *dimayon,* which means imagination.

So, we are not just *Homo sapiens,* we are *Homo imaginus.* Let's imagine together in an imagination exercise and imagine this into existence by imagining together in symphony:

I imagine an Evolutionary Church with hundreds of millions of people where everyone is finding what they want to give. We are vocationally aroused. We are finding each other.

> *Unique Self Symphony will*
> *be a passionate expression of*
> *vocational arousal.*

Let's take that phrase: *I see you. I love you.* No one evolves alone. **That is the nature of evolution. Evolution is interactive.**

We are part of a field, we get all the inputs of the field, we give back into the field.

THE INTERIOR TECHNOLOGY OF IMAGINATION

Let's just imagine a world of seeing each other with God's eyes. We are enacting the evolutionary impulse itself because the eyes of evolution open through us. These evolutionary eyes see problems and challenges that the government and the top-down system can't see.

We are giving our gifts as we see where they are needed and where we fit in as co-creators.

Whenever someone aroused to be God's eyes that arousal sends a ripple of arousal in their circle of intimacy and influence, and ever more gifts are given in this bottom-up Unique Self Symphony.

And then God joins through us. God joins through us! God awakens in us, as conscious Unique Selves arousing the very fabric of Reality itself.

And then what happens, beloveds? Then evolution itself becomes conscious of what it is, and everyone knows that we are evolution becoming conscious of the entire billions of years of genius.

Oh my God!

I am that I am. I am imagining an *Office for the Future* that connects what is working in the world, and that is so powerful that it transforms our political system.

Oh my God! I imagine that!

We imagine the memory of the future!

I am imagining us discovering the awesome potential of our world when we connect what is working.

I imagine us connecting and co-creating worldwide.

I imagine the news is no longer only the news of what isn't working. The news is about what *is* working!

I imagine turning on the news and there are going to be Outrageous Lovers on the news, and **we are going to be telling the stories of Unique Selves performing Outrageous Acts of Love.** Because we are Evolutionary Lovers, and what do Evolutionary Lovers do? They commit Outrageous Acts of Love that no one else can do. And I imagine the news reports on events happening in the Unique Self Symphony all over the world. People watch the news and they are not devastated by the abhorrent violence. They are actually blown wide open by the common good that is happening all the time.

We *are* the news! It is not only, *well, we will have to tell the news.* Each person alive is an emergent property of that God-force creating!

To be a Unique Self is to be the good news.

Because what does it mean to be a Unique Self? To be a Unique Self is to know that you are *newness*! *Newness* means something new that never was, is, or will be ever again. Reality intended every personal uniqueness; Reality intended your uniqueness. *Reality is*, said Alfred North Whitehead,[8] *the creative advance into novelty*, the newness that never was, is, or will be. Because you can see with Goddess's eyes in a way that no one else that ever was, is, or will be can ever do, you are newness and you are the news!

As Sri Aurobindo told us, *the supramental genius of universal creativity is showing up through us.*

Our genius is so much more when we are doing this together than when we are separate alone and competing.

We are the newness!

We are the revolution!

The words merge into each other because we are together, serving the evolutionary impulse, and we get to join genius. And the impulse appears uniquely as each one of us.

Here is the statement: To be an evangelist is to know **I am the *good news*, and you are the *good news*, and we are the *good news*.**

I get to be a lover. **To be a lover is to see with God's eyes,** meaning I get to see *you*, and I get to say, *Oh my God, I am blown away.* I realize Reality is having a *you experience.*

I don't say to myself, *Why am I not you ?* No, once I can let that go, I realize, *you are a Unique Self, and I am a Unique Self.* I get to be blown away by you,

---

8   Alfred North Whitehead (1861–1947) was a British mathematician and philosopher best known for his work in mathematical logic and the philosophy of science.

and then I get to be in love with you. Then I get to be in devotion to you. *I see you.* I am the *good news.*

Let's envision the planetary awakening in love through a Unique Self Symphony of each of us co-creating. Just imagine that the world is going to be a symphony of love. **It sounds idealistic, but it *is the most realistic* thing there is** because every one of us is *already* that.

Nature creates the whole system.

We can place a new vision in the Field of Evolution.

Nature creates through intention. Intention creates. Intention literally creates! Let's bring this kind of evangelical outburst—you are the *good news,* and I am the *good news,* and we are the *good news*—into a crystallized vision of intention, an Evolutionary Church that has developed new technologies.

PERSONAL SELF IS NEVER BYPASSED

Ecstasy means to be beside myself, but **it is not ecstasy in which I lose connection to the world, it is the ecstatic urgency of the evolutionary impulse** beating in us, saying, *we can overcome!*

- ◆ We can overcome the lethargy.
- ◆ We can overcome the entropy.
- ◆ We can overcome the depression.
- ◆ We can overcome and transform.

Everyone is enacting, creating, and weaving together. We are all weaving together.

To be in community together, to draw strength from each other, to feel each other, and to create this together is everything.

We are never bypassing the personal self.

It is always about *I want to know what love is*, and I want to know that love is Evolutionary Love. **All of our heartache and personal pain and all of our loneliness, it is not bypassed.** We raise it up, and we bring it to the altar. We know that everything is seen and everything is held.

We know that Reality is not a fact, my friends, it is a story. We know it is not an ordinary story, it is a love story. We know that **my love story is part of the love story of the Universe**, and that my heartache and pain is part of the love story. **My yearning is part of evolution's yearning.** And it all becomes a larger whole offered up in tears and joy.

We laugh out of one side of our mouth, and we cry out of the other side of our mouth.

As we sing and cry out our hymn, *I want to know what love is,*[9] we become it together.

We thank the story of Creation coming out through all of us, and we thank our opportunity to make the difference in the world. I am thankful for making the difference through the expression of co-creation, Evolutionary Love, and a world of massive vocational arousal.

Amen!

We are it and we know what love is! **The revolution is happening. We are loving it open.** What a delight and honor to be with you. Oh my God!

---

9   "I Want to Know What Love Is," by Foreigner.

CHAPTER FIVE
THE EVOLUTION OF POWER

Episode 55 — November 11, 2017

A NEW STORY OF POWER

We have a new story to tell. It is the story of creation. The story of creation is unfolding as you and me.

Let's just place our attention on the billions of years of that process of creation, which is conceived of as a process of greater love, of greater consciousness, of greater freedom, which is now encoded in you and me as our impulse to love. The power of this is awesome.

If we ever feel powerless, we just need to shift our attention to the power within and allow ourselves to feel the entire process of creation. **The way Creation creates is by attracting**—particle with particle, cell with cell, multi-cell with multi-cell, animal with animal, human with human.

The Evolutionary Church is coming into form at the moment of the evolutionary birth of humanity experiencing itself as a whole body.

We have seen ourselves from space. We are one planet.

We are feeling ourselves from within as the impulse of creation, and we are attracted to each other in the Evolutionary Church of creation. **We are expressing directly to each other the joy we feel when we are in**

resonance together, when we are awakening the story as it unfolds with us.

We are resonating inside. **We are a memory of the future**, and our resonance opens us up to be able to find that memory, and the *dharma* grounds us in that memory.

We are here to talk about power. The whole conversation here is about the evolution of power. We need a new narrative of power. **We need a new story of power.**

For instance, what is the entire conversation going on between North Korea and America? It's a kind of *power posturing*.

What is the entire tragedy of the Weinstein story? The abuse of power.

Who has power? Who doesn't have power? How do we claim our power?

We have interrogated power as a negative. **We have made power a bad thing**. We believe if you have power somehow that power must be in some sense abusive, **because we don't have a story of power. We don't have a narrative of power.**

What we are here to do is to articulate a narrative of power in which we begin to understand that power is not abuse. Misused power is abuse, but power is holy. Power is sacred.

There is a reason why the great traditions talked about God as the Infinity of Power, but in those traditions God was outside. And, yes, God remains the power that holds us; God remains the power in whose arms we can rest, and yet we realize that that power lives authentically in us, as it pulses through us.

70

If we don't have a narrative of power, which is an evolutionary narrative, an authentic narrative, in which we get to claim **the dignity and the delight and the devotion that emerges from the power flowing through us**, then the only thing that remains is a narrative which is about the pathology of power.

If we don't claim the delight of power, the holiness of power, then power pathologizes itself.

Power will not be denied.

Every human being has a right to the dignity of their power. And my good friend, Jimi Hendrix, he had a lot of things right, but he had one thing wrong. He made it an opposition between the love of power and the power of love.[10]

No, it is no opposition! The love of power is beautiful when I realize that **love is a form of power**. No opposition between love and power. There is pathological power and there is holy power.

One of the ways we know, my friends, that our power is holy is because we know that our lives matter, that our lives are dignified. We know that what we do in **our stories matters to God, matters to the Infinity of Intimacy,** which is the name for the Divine that we have coined.

The inside of power is intimacy.

And God is not merely the Infinity of Power, God is the Infinity of Intimacy. Our lives are dignified in prayer, and prayer affirms the dignity of personal need, because we matter, and our prayers matter. And God, Divinity, Reality, the Universe, is moved by our claiming the dignity of our personal need, which is the dignity of our power.

---

10   Jimi Hendrix said: "When the power of love overcomes the love of power, the world will know peace."

THE DIGNITY OF POWER ENDS VICTIMHOOD

Not to be dignified in our power is to be a victim, to be powerless. Why is victimhood problematic? Because, we felt powerless! That is the exact conversation here. We are saying: *Someone made me powerless.* But, the idea is not to remove all powers but to become empowered.

We become empowered because we claim the dignity of our story. We claim the dignity of the power of the evolutionary impulse moving in me.

And we realize that our lives matter to Infinity. And Infinity is looking at me and is saying:

> *Come closer. Come closer. Like this. You matter! Your story matters! Every detail of your story matters! Pray to me! Pray! Ask me! Be prayer!*
>
> *Bring to me every detail of your life!*
>
> *Bring to me your holy and your broken Hallelujah!*
>
> *Bring to me your crushed heart!*
>
> *Bring to me the injustice!*
>
> *Bring to me the lack of fairness, but not as a victim!*
>
> *Bring to me your holy and broken Hallelujah with full power!*

One of the reasons we love Leonard Cohen is because **he owns both the holy and the broken *Hallelujah* without being a victim.** [*See Appendix*]

Yes, of course we stand for victims in the world. And of course, all of us may have been victimized. But my identity is, *Oh my God, I have power!* **I have the power of the evolutionary impulse rising in me!**

I have Outrageous Acts of Love to commit. After I say *me too* and I affirm the parameters and boundaries of not violating my personal space—which is sacred, and we all stand for that here—after I say *me too*, I also say, Oh my God, *me Yes!*

72

And *me Yes* is the affirmation of the dignity of my story. That begins with prayer. The dignity of my power, the gorgeousness of my power is **not power over, but power for.** It is about empowering. It is about the dignity of power. The dignity of power begins with prayer, where we embrace the holy and the broken *Hallelujah*.

We know that every detail of our story matters, our power matters. And away we go.

Let's evolve the source code. Let's participate together in the very evolution of love, and we pray with the holy and the broken *Hallelujah*.

I AM PRAYER, I AM POWER

In prayer, we bring our intimacy. And prayer is intimacy. We are looking for intimacy. But the way we find our intimacy is to know every detail of our story matters. Feel in my prayer, my power, my dignity, I am king, I am queen, and I come before you, Divine, and I ask for everything. Let's ask for everything, let's ask for everything that I need, for everything that my neighbor needs, everything that my uncle needs, everything that my daughter needs. I say, *God, please!* Let's ask for everything.

I pray for everything, because I am in my power. Prayer is not an emasculation of power. **Prayer is power.** Move from being what the Greeks called a spectator to *being a prayer!*

I am prayer and I am power. Prayer and power are not separate.

There is no ego, there is no me. There is: I am prayer, I am power. We are the collective of evolution. We are in Florence bringing in modernity. We are the new church. We are in Bethlehem. Every person who writes it changes something in the source code. If you are willing to step in and respond to the divine voice that says:

> *Come closer, like this, I need you to write this in my heart, so we can evolve the source code together.* I am prayer. I am power. And can you hear Her saying, *Could a few more people write this in*

73

my heart? Can I feel all of you because you are me, and I am you, and when you write this in my heart, the source code evolves and so, can you come and write it?

Can you hear Her saying that? *Come closer—like this. Come closer—like this.*

Beloved whole mates, we evolve the source code together. Come closer!

OUR POWER IS SOURCED IN THE GARDENS OF INFINITE SOURCE

Yes, I come closer. I am the power. I am the story of creation.

The impulse within me to be more, to love more, create more *is* the power of evolution, and it and I are the power of evolution together.

I am including: I am the Universe expressing itself as me, through me, for me, and for everything in everyone as universal evolution.

That power is truly awesome. It is truly God.

What I am doing is taking one of the sentences and then playing with it. I am going to start out with the sentence, *We need a new story that is equal to our power.*

But really, we have a new story equal to our power. It is The Universe: A Love Story. It is evolution by attraction, all the way up and all the way down.

Let's affirm that we all have the story: The Universe: A Love Story.

Most specifically, *we need a new story of power itself.* The new story is a *narrative.* It is a *trajectory of power,* and I have been working with the word *trajectory* in regard to the new story. If you have a trajectory that is imbued with the power of evolution that means your narrative is empowered.

I have been consciously identifying my trajectory as starting with the origin of creation. I couldn't have made any of this up. In the actual present moment, that trajectory has the power of the whole story going somewhere.

Where does the trajectory or where does the narrative of evolution go? It goes to help us be more loving, more creative. It is what Teilhard de Chardin said:

- The story brings us greater consciousness.
- The story brings us greater freedom to say *Yes* or no.
- The story brings us greater synergistic love and joining to create.

This is another tremendous revelation: my deepest desire happens to be the Universe and me desiring it.

If you want to talk about feeling empowered—that really does it for you, but you have to get hold of your trajectory. It must personalize. It is not that I have the trajectory of billions of years of evolution, I have *my unique trajectory.* I have my love of the particular impulse. I have the trajectory of this church inside me. It shows up as the Evolutionary Unique Self. This is the great plan God had.

My yearning is showing up as my Evolutionary Unique Self, which is empowered by the entire process of creation.

Do you realize how awesome that is? To be that fully empowered?

Part of the evolution of consciousness is the evolution of our experiences and narrative of power.

As Evolutionary Unique Selves, we feel both powerful and humble beyond measure. We are powerful because the impulse of evolution itself pulses as us. In other words, we are accepting the power of evolution, *personally.*

We are humbled because we realize that **our power is sourced in the Garden of Infinite Source that lives us in every moment, and without which we would cease to exist.**

Sometimes I thought, *what if the whole thing turned off?* I mean, this is not just in you personally, but in the Universe, because whatever's going on in you personally is going on across the planet, across this Cosmos, in this entire universe.

We have to take the personal universally. It is a very, very great expansion of what is personal. Since I am really taking it as a universal impulse, I ask, *what does this infinite source in me yearn for?*

It is a passionate desire. It is a longing for greater intimacy, union, and co-creation with it and with each other. And, this is the thing about love: Love is this inner impulse for intimacy, which is the nature of the Universe to become and to seek greater intimacy.

What does that mean? Well, it is more than ordinary love, obviously. It's the love that creates through joining. It is GodLove joining. It's Godhood through us. It is awesomely great. It is the Infinite Source who lives in us as passionate desire, as longing for greater intimacy, union, and co-creation with It, and with each other.

Without a cogent narrative of power, an All-That-Is that is sacred—from relationships to purpose to sex—we lose our core ethos and Eros.

In other words, if you don't have this story, it everything else in your life. Your relationships, your love, your sexuality, your *ethos,* your luck—it is all gone!

When we are impelled and realize where the source of this passion comes from, it is inevitably truthful.

It is not that we can't make mistakes with it. We can, but its intimacy and its power are so empowering that you cannot fail.

You cannot fail with this inside you. **The core ethics is a trajectory towards your and my heart's desire.** This means, you really have to take your heart's desire seriously.

It is not enough to say: *Oh well, this is my personal heart's desire.*

One thing I (Barbara) think that conscious evolution has done for me, is to make me realize that my heart's desire is the universal process within me desiring, and when it hits a crisis, or something that it doesn't know how to resolve or feels at a loss, I have learned to say, *thank you, what are you pointing me towards?*

This is true personally; it is true socially, and it is true on a planetary scale. We now have problems that look like we can't quite solve them. This is absolutely true! We can't solve them unless we evolve in consciousness, freedom, and order. The Universe is pressing us through these crises, every single one of them, starting personally and all the way up to climate change and nuclear holocaust.

We have been given exactly the degree of struggle that we need to be as exactly great as we can be when we incarnate this power.

There is a drive for core intimacy, greater expression of genius, longing for sexual union, longing for supra-sexual union, longing for whole mate-ing. In this church, we are whole mate-ing wherever we can find a place to join genius for shared purpose.

There's no more wonderful love than whole mate-ing—joining genius for shared purpose, toward the purpose of evolution itself, which is greater consciousness, freedom, and loving order—to see how the Divine has entered into the personal.

YOUR DESIRE IS EVOLUTION'S DESIRE

And what happens if you are celibate? I just wanted to mention Teilhard de Chardin here. As a Catholic, obviously he was celibate, and he *really* loved a woman. And she *really* loved him. I have wondered how that worked. Here is what I did learn about it, because I worked closely with the sisters of St. Joseph, a Catholic order. One of them, sister Judy Colley, was an evolutionary. She absolutely loved this whole story. She told me what those sisters did, and I think it is a practice that we could all use.

Those sisters, when they were over in Europe, decided to come to this new country by themselves. They had no bishop. They came in threes, as little threesomes of these Catholic sisters in the new country. Every morning they had a meeting and asked themselves two questions:

- What is the state of your heart?
- What is the order of the house?

And those threesomes of Catholic nuns came and populated the planet. I was one of their sisters. They asked me when I had become Catholic. And since I wasn't Catholic, I said, *I am not Catholic. But why do you think I am Catholic?* And they said, *Because you have such a great sense of expectation.*

A lot of the other religions do not have this sense of expectation.

Thinking of the Second Coming of Christ, when we are talking here about the planetary awakening in love through a Unique Selves Symphony, that is pretty close to that. That was those nuns' form of intimacy.

The sexual energy, as they realized it, can be carried into the evolutionary trajectory, becoming one with the narrative of evolution itself.

THE EVOLUTION OF POWER

Wow. The evolutionary story of creation really needs to be brought out into the general public, and the new story of love needs to be told on CNN because it's ridiculous that we have to hear nothing but pathetic love stories of men and women seeking power through sex.

Your desire, your longing, is evolution longing inside of you.

We have such an opportunity to talk about Evolutionary Love in the public arena. Some might warn, *be careful, watch out, they will try to annihilate you.*

Maybe.

But how many of us are there? How important is our voice now to be heard through all the ways in which we can communicate?

We are at a whole new phase of the narrative of power.

THE RIGHT PLACE AND THE RIGHT TIME TO STEP INTO POWER

Let us step into the new story.

What are the words that we want to speak?

What is this new narrative of power that we are here together to talk about and articulate with all of us?

Let's try to articulate the new narrative of power.

PREMODERNITY'S NARRATIVE OF POWER

In premodernity, meaning until the Renaissance, where was the power?

- The power was outside.

- God had the power.
- Human beings had no power.
- The only job of human beings was to bow to God's power.

If there was a king who had power, what did we call it?

We called it the *divine right of kings*, meaning the king only had a power because God said, *You have power*. And God was outside the world.

There were two circles, the world and God. God is outside the world. Human beings by definition are not God, therefore they don't have power.

That is the end of the story.

Power is with God. Obedience was the core, tragically, of the Catholic message. And the sisters mentioned above were revolutionaries within the Catholic Church. But the core Catholic message was God has the power, grace is with God. **It is only by absolute faith that you have grace. Therefore, you are essentially emasculated**. That was the story.

MODERNITY'S NARRATIVE OF POWER

Along came the Renaissance. The Renaissance said: No, no, we must take power back from God. Think of Michelangelo's *David*, in Florence. It is the human's creation, the human creativity, and the human initiative.

The Renaissance was Prometheus unbound. Let's steal the fire from heaven. Let's tell the story of Prometheus. So now, where does power rest? With the individual! That is what the Renaissance says. That's not premodernity; that's modernity. Power rests with the individual.

But all of a sudden, we had another version of the same tragedy! The human being was alienated from Source, alienated from the Divine. All the power rests with the individual separate self, and even any power that the government had came from the social contract. Which meant that individuals gave up power for the sake of the government having a little power, but there is no intrinsic power.

Intrinsic power lives in only one place; it lives only with the individual.

But my friends, how much power can an individual have?

An individual as a skin-encapsulated ego, as Gregory Bateson was going to call it a few hundred years later, doesn't have much power.

That means that I have to get my power at your expense. I have to steal power from you. Which is why Hobbes at the beginning of modern political theory said the world is always in a natural state of war. People are just stealing power from each other, and my power comes at your expense. Power is a zero-sum game.

Therefore, power is pathological, but is also the nature of the human being in life, which is nasty, brutish and short. **Modernity's vision of power** was that:

- Power is limited to the separate self.
- There is no source power that lives in the human being.
- Human beings are in a natural state of war.

It is always about surrounding my property with a moat and a wall, so *I will be defended in my boundaries. If anyone violates my boundaries, that is the most dangerous thing in the world.* We get that.

That's the beauty, the dignity, of modernity—and it's also the disaster of modernity.

POSTMODERNITY'S NARRATIVE OF POWER

Along comes postmodernity and says: *Oh my god, even the modern stories of individual rights are really hidden grabs for power.*

Postmodernity saw that everyone is trying to grab power in different ways, while there are all these disempowered people at the margins. Let's bring them in—lesbians, the gay community, LGBTQ—that is gorgeous!

Postmodernity saw that the Earth has been ignored! We are raping the Earth. Let's bring the Earth in, the environment! That is fantastic, gorgeous!

Postmodernity says, **there are all these power grabs that are victimizing everyone**.

Let's expose the power grabs and bring in all the people who were victimized.

That is gorgeous! That is a momentous leap in history.

But, there is no narrative of power.

THE NEW NARRATIVE IS: I AM POWER!

Until we come to this moment in time, there was no narrative of power. We proclaim the new narrative of power.

The new narrative power is to say, *I am power.*

I am power, because the source of power itself, the evolutionary impulse, uniquely expressed as me, pulses and beats and throbs in me.

I am not merely a separate self. I am not the Renaissance skin-encapsulated ego. The world is not Shakespeare, *a tale told by an idiot, full of sound and fury, signifying nothing*. Rather, *I am the power and we are the power*. Let's get both of them:

- I am an expression, a unique expression of the Field.
- I am an irreducible Unique Self.
- I am an Evolutionary Unique Self.
- I live in an evolutionary context.
- The evolutionary impulse pulses uniquely in me.

- I am not separate self. I don't just have power as separate self.
- I have power as a unique expression of the Field, the one field of True Self.
- I am an Evolutionary Unique Self, meaning evolution pulses uniquely in me, irreducibly in me.

And what is evolution? Evolution is that force driven by Evolutionary Love.

Evolutionary Love powers the whole story. It means:

- I am a unique expression of Evolutionary Love.
- I am a unique expression of the Evolutionary Love impulse of the Cosmos.
- The codes that we are unfolding here are the Evolutionary Love Codes.
- I am the power.
- I am the evolutionary love power of Reality uniquely expressed as me.

Once I get that, I get to claim my power. When I feel power coursing through me, and I feel my desire for power, I feel like I want to show up; I want to wake up; I want to grow up; I want to give my gift; I want to be Superman!

I want to find and identify my superpowers, and I go to my therapist and my therapist says: *That is grandiosity, that is grandiosity.* I am pathologized.

My desire for power is pathologized.

But I do know. I just watched Superman. I just went to Wonder Woman. How many women went to Wonder Woman and said: *Oh my god, hello, that is me, that is my incarnation!* And all women *should* claim Wonder Woman, and all men *should* claim Superman, because that is the truth. We do have superpowers, we are superheroes with superpowers, and my Unique Self is the unique superpowers that live in me.

I am Wonder Woman. I am Superman. I am power.

Then we come together as a Unique Self planetary awakening in love. A planetary awakening in Evolutionary Love comes together Unique Self synergies.

Synergy means we come together to form a whole larger than the sum of its parts.

The greatest Unique Self synergy is the Unique Self Jazz Symphony. And why is it a jazz symphony? Because I never know what note you are going to play. And I never know what note another player is going to play.

I am in the Symphony. How do I come together with you and give up some of myself so I can listen to your music that is going to make my music better?

I am power! I am Wonder Woman, I am Superman, and **together we are the league of superheroes.**

That is us, the league of superheroes. We are the Unique Self Symphony. We are the power. Can we find that?

We are the power! We have gone from *I am the power* to *We are the power.* That is when it happens. We are the power. **We are writing source code texts**.

We are the software engineers of Reality, participating in this moment in the evolution of love, feeling the power.

Can you feel that power coursing through you in this moment? That is not weak, that is not insipid. That is the power.

The evangelist brings the good news, and the good news is: we are the power.

And if we are not the power, then Trump is the power.

You get it?

The universe doesn't tolerate a vacuum of power. We *are* the power. And we have to own our drive for power. Because our drive for power is holy and it is beautiful.

When we don't own our drive for power, when we distance ourselves, when we split it off from ourselves, then our drive for power appears pathologically.

It appears pathologically, and we are willing to compromise everything for a moment of fifteen minutes of fame. That is the pathology of power.

We want the purity of power. We are the power, the purity of power, the potency of power, the poignant beauty of power.

Amen!

Let's feel this together.

Be grand! This is not grandiosity! You are the power! We are the power!

POWER LIVES IN THE PRIVATE MOMENTS WHEN WE DECIDE TO STAND IN INTEGRITY

The power in each of us is also our calling, our creativity, our vocation, our life purpose. When we say, *I am the power,* I am also the creative impulse. That *is* the power!

Everybody is looking for exactly how to best express the power. I just want to emphasize the enormity of that need to express the power uniquely as you.

When we say, *I am the power*, we don't mean *I am pathological power*. We mean *I am called to give my unique gift, which is my unique expression of the LoveIntelligence and LoveBeauty that is the power.*

That is the power that seeks to live through me and **as long as that power doesn't live through me, I will be in pain.** I really want to get that: all the Prozac in the world will not give you the power. The power will give you something that Prozac will not. I am not saying not to use Prozac, if that works, whatever helps you to balance and stabilize, use that absolutely, that is fabulous. Stabilize always. But, my friends, Prozac will not give us the potency and the poignancy and the power that creates the purity of a life well lived, and **a life well lived is to say, *I am living my power*,** and my power is not anyone else's power.

My power is *my* power.

Reality is having a *me* experience, but Reality is having a *you* experience at the same time.

Power is not about being public. That is where Andy Warhol had it wrong. Power is not about 15 minutes of fame.

I really want to get this: power is not public.

Sometimes power is public, but power at its core is private. Private means, how do I show up when no one is watching? How do I show up in the integrity of my life?

My vocation is not simply my public gift. My vocation is the gift of my integrity in the private moments where all of my family tells me not to do it, when I could get away with not doing it. There are always good reasons not to be it, not to commit the Outrageous Acts of Love that are mine to commit.

Don't translate *power* into *public*. Power sometimes needs to be public. The Evolutionary Church needs to be public. But my friends, power at its core is heroic.

---

*Heroism—like Superman and
Wonder Woman at their core—shows
in the private moments of our lives,
when we decide to stand in integrity,
even though we can totally get away
politically with not doing it.*

That is where power lives.

That is where integrity lives.

That is where we become empowered in a way that no one can take it away from us. And I want to tell you something with enormous pathos. Do you think Jesus on the cross was powerful? I think he was. Crucified.

Let's go from crucifixion to resurrection, it is time for resurrection! It is not time for crucifixion.

But I want to tell you something. Would Jesus have been more powerful if he did not walk the way to the cross and went instead to Jerusalem and dined with the powerful people in Jerusalem in the establishment of that moment, it would have looked more powerful, but he wouldn't have been.

Jesus's power and Isaiah's power was to speak truth to pathological power.

That is true power.

To take risks, and to risk the whole mission for a moment of integrity, and not to be too strategic but to have holy audacity.

Holy audacity!

You know, when God says, when Infinity of Intimacy says, *come closer like this*, She is not looking for the public display of a Wonder Woman kind of landing with that awesome outfit and the entire world watching.

Heroic moments are almost always private. And you can always get away with not doing them, and no one is going to call you out on them.

But watch, even in the spiritual world, we can commodify spirit, we can commodify public.

It has to live in private.

When it lives in private, then it explodes in the public. And the power, my friends, of Evolutionary Church is that we love each other in private.

- ◆ We talk to each other.
- ◆ We find each other in the chats.
- ◆ We find each other in Outrageous Love Letters.
- ◆ We find each other and study together.
- ◆ We stand in this private crucible of loving, and from there we explode, and from there we know we are the power.
- ◆ And from there we look in each other's eyes, and we say, *come closer, like this! Beloved, I am here*, and then we are all resurrected.

Oh my God. Oh my God!

CHAPTER SIX

WE ARE GOD'S UNIQUE INTIMACY AND GOD'S POWER

Episode 56 — November 18, 2017

EVOLUTIONARY LOVE CODE: GOD IS THE INFINITY OF INTIMACY

God is not only the Infinity of Power, God is the Infinity of Intimacy.

WE ARE GOD'S UNIQUE INTIMACY OF POWER

God is not only the Infinity of Power, God is the Infinity of Intimacy. We are God's unique intimacy.

Let's just dwell for a moment in the *Infinity of Power*: think of an infinite Universe.

Within that infinite Universe, in the first explosion of power, in that Big Bang, in that Infinity, was the absolute precision of every particle that could make matter, energy, life, and us.

The power to be able to create an entire Universe with the Infinity of Intimacy through every particle being

attracted by allurement to each other—love at the very core of the Infinity of Intimacy and Power—is such an awesome plan.

We are God's unique intimacy, which would also mean we are God's unique intimacy of power that is held in that infinity of our intimacy.

This identity of the human and God in the resonant field can only be experienced if we release the illusion of separation.

Let's resonate with the entire story of Creation and feel that impulse of evolution as God's Infinity of Power residing exactly as God's unique intimacy in you and me—now.

It is an awesome, magnificent experience.

Holding it together now as a WeSpace. It is easier to hold it, if you are in a WeSpace than if you are just alone. We are holding it as WeSpace here in this Evolutionary Church right now.

We are God's unique intimacy in person, resonating with each other exactly at this frequency, holding it in a steady state long enough for it to imprint our nervous systems. We're in a resonant field, each person re-sounding the unique intimacy of God—both within us and collectively.

We are here to love it open.

We want to just state the code once more, and I remember I wrote the first version of this code in Unique Self, when I was trying to understand how we move beyond being just a unique perspective. That is how the Unique Self work began.

I am a True Self.

I am *part* of The One, but I don't *disappear* into The One.

I have a unique perspective. Everyone has a unique perspective.

Everyone is located at a unique place in the space-time continuum.

My True Self plus my unique perspective equals my Unique Self. That is how we began. But then, just to share with everyone, it *bothered* me. **We are more than a unique perspective!** Unique perspective was too clinical, too rigorous. And I began to feel, well, what is this *you-ness*? What is this *me-ness*?

I am a unique quality of intimacy.

I am a unique taste. I don't get confused about who is standing before me. There is a unique taste of each one of us.

We each have a unique quality of intimacy, and I realized, oh my God, we are God's unique intimacy! We are going to put it all together:

Conscious Evolution and God's unique intimacy are one teaching.

ARE YOU READY TO PLAY A LARGER GAME?

We are here to love it open for the sake of the evolution of love.

We ask ourselves, *are you, are we, am I, ready to play a larger game?*

Are you ready to participate in the evolution of love?

That is the question we ask all the time. And it is the question I have asked in wisdom school for ten years, and you ask the question like this: *are you ready to awaken as the impulse to be more, to love more?* These are other beautiful formulations of the same question.

- Are you ready to be more, to love more, to awaken as the impulse?
- Are you ready to play a larger game?
- Are you ready to participate in the evolution of love?

We **want to love *Reality itself* open**. And how do we do that? We are literally in Bethlehem. We are the new church. We are at the place that da Vinci was in Florence.

Like in premodernity during the Black Death when the plague wiped out so much of the world, the whole world today, in postmodernity is fragmenting.

We are about to grow exponentially to an extent that we are going to fall off the cliff with using up resources, overpopulation, dying of the seas, methane gas evaporation in the tundra, rogue terrorist bombs.

We need to change the story!

Those are not just words.

We are facing existential threat of the kind that we have never seen before, with the actual capacity to destroy ourselves. **We need a story equal to our power.** We need a love story equal to our power. We need an understanding of Reality equal to our power.

We are participating in the evolution of consciousness and culture, which is the evolution of love.

IN PRAYER, WE RE-PATTERN REALITY

In order to get into prayer, we need to re-understand what prayer is. We used to understand that God was the Infinity of Power and that God lived outside of us. Now, we still think, based on the best evolutionary science and interior science, that Rumi wasn't wrong. Let's get this straight. We are going to re-correct, we are going to re-pattern here.

We are going to re-pattern Reality. **We are re-patterning the source code of Reality.** We feel—because that is the deep truth of inner realization—that we are held.

Rumi falls into the arms of the beloved. There is a divine intelligence that existed before the human neocortex, that manifested mitosis and meiosis.

We are held by the Divine.

Oh my God, we are held! The Divine that lives beyond us. The Divine that is the Infinity of Power, of which supernovas are but a pale reflection.

What we want to say here together intimately—because to join genius is intimate—we want to say together that God is not just the Infinity of Power, God is not just beyond us, God is the Infinity of Intimacy. And this is a core foundation stone of the Evolutionary Church.

> *The evolution of God is when we, the God in us, understands, realizes divinity in an entirely new way.*

Oh my God!

God is not merely the Infinity of Power. God is the Infinity of Intimacy.

My friends, if you are not jumping off your seat, if you are not like flipping your heart out, if I am not flipping my heart out, then we did not get it!

This is a source code moment!

Be intimate together. We are a *Field of We*. God is not only the Infinity of Power. God is the Infinity of Intimacy. God is the Infinity of Intimacy, and each one is God's unique intimacy. That is the resonant field. Oh my God.

There is a quality of intimacy that is *you-ness*. Then, if two people come together and join genius, which is when each single person meets God's unique intimacy in the other, a new intimacy is created, which also means that **a new God has been created.**

That is not metaphor. That is not poetry!

That is ontology. That is true!

And when we come together and participate, and our unique intimacy shows up in the Field, we are playing a bigger game.

All of a sudden, we create a larger Field of Intimacy, which is a new expression of the Divine. The church *is* God, but not in the hijacking of God, not in the ethnocentric way, not in the dogma way, but in the realization: **God is the Infinity of Intimacy that knows our name.**

Let me ask you a question: if you or I are awake in the middle of the night and we are lonely, does God know? Of course, She does!

God is the Infinity of Intimacy.

God is intimate with us! Isaiah says it so beautifully:

> In all of your contraction, in all of your pain, I am with you. I am with you in the narrow places. I am with you in your holy Hallelujah, and I am with you in your broken Hallelujah.

I just need you to realize every breath you draw is *Hallelujah*. *Hallelujah* means God is the Infinity of Intimacy. *Hallelujah* is not only divine, pristine praise, *hallel*—ecstasy.

Hallelujah is the broken intoxication, it is the shattered vessels and the shattered hearts, and it is the lonely places, and it is the yearning places, and it is the contracted places that live in all of us.

Who we are is not New Age caricatures of ourselves, who bypass pain and contraction. It is our ability to walk through the contraction, to be in it for ten minutes, and then to come out gloriously on the other side in full power, in full dignity.

It means to not murder each other from the contraction, but to love the contraction open into the expanse of space of walking together in the wide places.

We turn to the Divine, the divine God who knows your name, who knows every thought that goes through your head, and every feeling that goes through your body, who knows my name, and who also *is* uniquely expressed as *you-ness*, each one's unique *you-ness*. In God's unique intimacy in every man and woman, and in the space between them, a new God is created.

This is the new God that is desperately needed to articulate a new narrative of power. *How do power and intimacy come together*, that is what we want to talk about.

We are participating together as activists. As mystical evolutionary activists playing a larger game, we are standing at the brink of the abyss, and we are saying:

- We are the evolution of love.
- We are evolution.
- We are the power.
- We are the intimacy.
- We are our holy and our broken *Hallelujah*.

We can't bypass it. It is only when we bypass the broken *Hallelujah*, when we deny the contraction, then we can't love it open, and then we murder each other from the place of the narrowness.

When we *embrace* the holy and broken *Hallelujah*, we know that every place we fall, we fall into Her arms. We know that She is always in he, in thee, and together, we come together as this holy we. Then, oh my God, we become a Unique Self Symphony of intimacy, participating in the evolution of love.

NECESSITY TO INFUSE TECHNOLOGICAL POWER WITH LOVE

I (Barbara) want to take a moment to describe what I learned about the Infinity of Power as it was gained by humans. To say God is the Infinity of

Power and that we are joining God in that Infinity, is one thing to say, but what has happened over the past 30, 40, 50 years is, **we have gained powers that we used to attribute to gods.**

A few notes from my book, *Conscious Evolution*, about how this happened. One text is from a great scientist from MIT, a professor at the Massachusetts Institute of Technology named Eric Chaisson who wrote about technology.

Remember, we are still talking about the Infinity of Power, and we now look at the power we have, while **we are sitting here in Evolutionary Church on the internet like holograms talking to each other.**

Chaisson says, *Technologically competent life differs fundamentally from lower forms of life, because we have learned to tinker not only with matter, but with evolution.*

We are saying evolution is the Infinity of God. This means that we're tinkering with the way God works—and God gave us this power to tinker.

Chaisson continues: *Technology, for all its pitfalls, enables life to begin to control matter, as much as matter evolved to control radiative energy more than ten billion years ago.*

Let's put ourselves in this story of the Infinity of Intimacy at the Big Bang. Let's look at that moment in those first few seconds, when God was able to infuse extraordinary capacities of organization in two or three seconds, that could form quarks, matter, and lifeforms, that were attracted by allurement, all the way on up to us.

Eric Chaisson calls us to enter a "mature life era." He says: *Our generation on planet Earth, as well as any other neophyte technological lifeform populating the universe, is now participating in an astronomically significant transformation. We perceive the dawn of a whole new reign of cosmic development.*

We have been talking about the Infinity of Intimacy as God's trajectory, and there are phases in this, as we have pointed out.

Chaisson continues: *The implications of our newly gained power over matter are nothing short of cosmic. As sentient beings, we are currently beginning to exert a weighty influence in the establishment of a universal life.*

One thing I want to comment here is that we happen to be alive, when we are *just beginning* to establish a new form of life.

Think *how immensely important* it is that **the Infinity of Intimacy and Love infuses that cosmic life with love.**

That is the power that we have right now.

The capacity for conscious evolution means that our species has become capable of understanding, resonating with, and consciously incarnating the process of creation itself.

The question here is our relationship to God.

It has shifted as God has given us the power to co-evolve, taking that Infinity of Intimacy within ourselves, and creating cosmic life here.

I (Barbara) am going to read a little phrase from a Catholic scholar, Beatrice Bruteau, from a passage called *Holy Technology*. I am doing this because technology looks to so many of us as alien and separate, and it can be.

But *we are technology*; our hand is technological genius.

Bruteau says, *From having felt completely at the mercy of the natural world, we begin gradually to feel in a position of power over the natural world.*

Now, we are concerned about that because we can destroy forests; we can destroy our environment, but we have been given this power. We talk about the Infinity of Power.

She says, *There are now producing beings that can so intelligently and freely and creatively manipulate the natural world*, in other words, we have been created as a form of nature that can affect what we have called the natural world.

We are a new form of nature right here.

Bruteau writes: *We ourselves are products of the self-making world, and what we do by our technologies is continue the self-making of this world.*

Let's infuse everything we are learning about technological power with love. If we can do that, we are taking God power purposely.

Now, on the history of quantum change, I read you one little quote from Tim Leary. He says, *The DNA code contains the blueprint of the past and the future; the caterpillar DNA contains the design for construction and operation of the butterfly body, so geneticists are just now discovering unused sections of the DNA, masked by histones and activated by non-histone proteins, which are thought to create the blueprint of the future.*

I want to state that those of us who are coded with this Infinity of Power need to create and to play the largest possible game, and that we better know what this coding in us is!

COSMOLOGY, CRISIS, CAPACITY

I am going to conclude this idea with what I call **the three C's**. It is an idea easy to remember. It applies to this new phase that we are in only since the 1960s, and in fact, none of our political systems are built on it, none of our religious systems are built on it, except here at this church.

The first C is the new cosmology.

This is interesting to remember. This is a quote by Theodore Roszak in *The Voice of the Earth*:

> *The universe has altered radically over time.* (He is just saying this as a new perception.) *It has a history. These findings, the background radiation, the quasar, the Big Bang, and later Stephen Hawking's research on black holes, rapidly has coalesced with quantum mechanics and Einstein's relativity to produce a radically new picture.*

Einstein thought it was an eternal universe.

It wasn't until the 1960s when these radio astronomers discovered the background radiation of the original explosion. In one of the greatest scientific discoveries of the entire universe, according to Brian Swimme— and I think this is right—our scientists were able to map the evolutionary spiral from the Big Bang to us being here right now.

We add to what the scientific community does by giving it meaning, direction, purpose, and love.

So, the first C is the discovery.

The second C is the discovery of crises that could destroy the world.

We never have had crises at the scale of destroying our entire life-support system, of destroying all species that could exist, of destroying possibly the human species quickly.

---

*It is very important, if we are the
Infinity of God's Power, that we are
living right now during the crisis.*

I don't need to name all these crises to you, because you know them well, but they are evolutionary drivers of the highest order for the Infinity of Love.

The third C is the new capacities.

The new capacities are coming along at the same time as the new crises, just after the discovery of the Big Bang!

Our new capacities, powers now available to us such as biotechnology, nuclear power, nanotechnology, cybernetics, artificial intelligence, artificial life, are radical evolutionary capacities, potentially dangerous in our current state of self-centered consciousness. They may look unnatural, and indeed they are, yet if we consider our needs at the next stage of evolution—to restore the Earth, to free the people, and to explore the universal dimension of Reality—it could well be that we have been given these powers to be born as a universal species.

This little chapter ends with the requirement to learn conscious evolution.

How are we practicing conscious evolution with love when humanity could go either into radical devolution or radical evolution?

We have called it over and over a planetary awakening in love through a Unique Self Symphony on the internet. We are on the internet now! We are adding to the noosphere now!

I am longing for us to become sufficiently coherent in that internet as the nervous system of our planetary body. We are starting right here by speaking it—and by feeling it and by loving each other—and by infusing this living system with our love and with our power.

The *how-to* is a really great question that I am raising for all of us.

Evolutionary Church may be the one convening of people currently on this Earth with this cosmological impulse to co-create at an evolutionary scale. Everything is inherent in it.

HEALING THE SPLIT BETWEEN INTIMACY AND POWER

This is about power.

We want to **bring power and intimacy together.** We are introducing, writing together, the new source code. We have a great shared commitment which brought us together to join impulses, which is, *let's evolve the source code of what it means to be a human being,* which means to become *a new human!*

Whatever the language.

Here we say: *let's evolve the source code and become the new person, the new Self, the new human.* Others talk about *awakening the species.*

It is all the same thing.

That is our primary intention, and that is our shared intention. Out of that, there are lots of different pieces. There are lots of different pieces of that, but **the core intention is a shared impulse**. It is all of our shared impulse, because anyone who is in this church is here because we are allured to what I like to call the field of allurement that draws us.

In Hebrew, we have scripture on this, in the Song of Songs, the word for will—what is my will?

How do I act?

What is my will?

The word for will is *ratz,* and *ratz* means also *attraction* and *allurement.*

My will is formed by clarifying my allurement and moving from pseudo-allurement, from pseudo-eros—which is every form of addiction and every form of busyness—to the genuine allurement of realizing and feeling myself as part of the great Field of Allurement, and a unique expression which is God's unique intimacy.

Now, here is the paradox, and this is wild and beautiful, and feel how these things come together as we are the new human. We actually realize, oh my God, I am an electric cord, and at the end of that electric cord is a plug, and that plug is my Unique Self, and that Unique Self plugs into the field, and from that field, I draw my power.

Now, my power comes through my unique intimacy. In other words:

When I am in my Unique Self, when I am intimate with my allurement, I am in power.

I am empowered to act; I am empowered to transform; I am empowered to impact.

All of us want to be Wonder Woman. I want to be Superman, but I can only be Wonder Woman and Superman when I realize that God is not only the Infinity of Power, but the Infinity of Intimacy. And myself **as a human being, as a *Homo imago dei,* in the image of God, I am both filled with power and filled with intimacy.** When power and intimacy contradict each other, my life falls apart.

When we seek to have *power over* and not *power for*, we violate boundaries in sexual harassment; we seek to cover over the emptiness in a sexuality that is not filling us with love, which is the crisis we have in the world today.

When we have *power for*, we feel the power of all of Reality circling through that field, which is Unique Self filling us up with this gorgeous power, which is intimacy.

It is so stunning.

When we are in the depth of our power, our true power, our authentic power, we are in our authentic intimacy.

When we are in the depth of our authentic intimacy, we are in our authentic power.

We have this strange idea that we think that to be intimate, we have to be vulnerable in a way in which we become powerless. No! When we become intimate, we become transparent to the true power of Reality that is flowing through us.

There is no separation.

> *When we are in our intimacy, we become transparent to the power of Reality flowing through us.*

Our sentence is: **We are God's unique intimacy.**

We are God's unique intimacy. I am God's unique intimacy. *I am God's unique intimacy.*

Friends, I want you to hear this for a second. You can be in church on the stands, or you can get on the court. On the stands, you are listening. You are saying, *oh, that was a really nice insight. That was really great.* I am on the stands, but when I step into saying and writing *I am God's unique intimacy*, I am on the court. **In life, one of two things happen: You are either on the stands, or you are in the court.** The players—even if it is a boring game—have to stay, they can't leave before the end. They are on the court, right? The spectators, the fans—they are *fans.* But we are on the court. We are on the court together.

Now, from the place of being God's unique intimacy, flow all the way into the power. From being *I am God's unique intimacy*, take the intimacy now into the power, and write now: *I am the power.*

103

We are the power.

We go from God's unique intimacy into the power, so we have the actual experience of moving intimacy into power, and we rewrite the source code.

We are evolving the source code.

We are birthing the new human. We are inscripting this on the lips of the Divine that lives in us and lives beyond us. We are the power, not as separate self, not as contracted ego, not as grasping. We are the power. We are birthing the new human right now.

We go from intimacy to power, and for the first time, we are healing. In the very source code of everything, we are healing the split between intimacy and power.

We are awakening the new humanity. We are birthing the new human in this moment as we heal the split. We are this now. We are on the court. *I am the power. I am the power.* If you are up for it, if you are in, if you are out of the stands and on the court. *I am the power.* Find yourself intimate with God right now. We are this now. We are awakening the new human.

It is in the doing that it happens. Our power transforms the world. When we pray our individual prayer with the song, "I Want to Know What Love Is," I am praying for intimacy. But then I want that intimacy to fill not just me, but to fill everything, because we are the power.

We come together. *We are the power.* We are the power! We are the power, and we come together in the Field, and we step out into the court.

Amen.

Intimacy and power. Intimacy and power come together. The Infinity of Power met the Infinity of Intimacy.

Amen.

CHAPTER SEVEN

ALLUREMENT, INTIMACY, AND EVOLUTION

Episode 57 — November 25, 2017

EVOLUTION IS THE DEEPENING OF INTIMACY

Evolution is a trajectory of ever deepening intimacy. You go inside and feel the uniqueness of your being, feel it as God within you *uniquely* as you. Feel its qualities for a moment just as you, uniquely, awesomely, greatly, beautifully. It is God in you and as you.

Feel God as the frequency in you, joining you in ever greater intimacy.

Reach God in the uniqueness of you and bring all of the multiple levels of uniqueness into the ecstasy of intimacy within yourself, and with its super-personal or intimate person being revealed in all its glory and resonance.

We in this process which is not joining genes, but joining genius.

Another expression for it is to be *whole mates,* but it means the same thing.

We are wildly excited to be able to share this in the world. To be able to share what happens when people meet, and they realize that their evolutionary impulse is shared and they can therefore join not genes, but genius.

By genius we don't mean IQ level, we mean the gorgeous unique sharing and insight of two unique intimacies. That was our previous code: *You are God's unique intimacy*—two unique intimacies come together!

- We live in an Intimate Universe.
- You are God's unique intimacy.
- God is not just the Infinity of Power, but God is also the Infinity of Intimacy.

We are putting the Evolutionary Love Codes together. *We live in an Intimate Universe; God is not just the Infinity of Power, but the Infinity of Intimacy,* and *You are God's unique intimacy.*

The next code is:

EVOLUTIONARY LOVE CODE: THE EVOLUTION OF INTIMACY

Evolution is the process of ever increasing intimacy.

The trajectory of evolution is the evolution of intimacy.

How does that happen? It happens when intimacies come together, and a new configuration is formed.

If Reality having an intimate *me* experience meets Reality having an intimate *you* experience, and if there is a unique set of allurements— meaning not *all* quarks get together, and not *all* atoms get together—that says *let's join genius* (not genes), *let's join genius and bring together these two unique qualities of intimacy,* then **a new WeSpace is created**.

That is called an evolutionary WeSpace.

Oh my God!

An evolutionary WeSpace is when two separate intimacies that are part of the larger Field of Intimacy—meaning they are not ultimately separate—**come together and join genius to create a new emergent, a new synergistic emergent which is a new God!**

If God is not just the Infinity of Power, but the Infinity of Intimacy, and two intimacies come together to create a new WeSpace, or a new intimacy, that means a new God is being formed.

For example, when we come together in Evolutionary Church, together like da Vinci did with his cohorts in Florence, we create a new Field of Intimacy in which everyone's unique intimacy is on the table and everyone's unique gifts are on the table and everyone's unique voice is on the table and we create this new space.

Then the church becomes a new God, but not in the old dogmatic sense of the Catholic church, but in the sense of **beyond dogma.**

It is a Reality. It is an ontology.

We are a new emergent.

- ◆ We are a new expression.
- ◆ We are a new delight.
- ◆ We are a new quality of intimacy that never was ever before.

That is stunning! That is exciting!

PRAYER, AUTHENTIC NEED AND INTIMACY

We now turn in prayer. When we turn in prayer, we are turning in prayer as public prayer, as a church, synagogue, mosque, and it is not just the prayer of the individual.

It is not just that we are praying *in the community*, but we are praying *as the community*. When we pray as the community, the individual doesn't

get lost. It is not just communion. It is communion and autonomy at the same time.

We are individuals, gorgeous unique expressions of intimacy.

We turn to the Divine—again who is not just the Infinity of Power, but the Infinity of Intimacy—and we offer before God, as Rumi writes, we offer before the Beloved, who knows our name, who is intimate with our holy and our broken *Hallelujah*, we offer before God, who is the Infinity of Intimacy, who loves us madly in this Intimate Universe and who wants to receive our deepest need and to know our deepest need, we offer what we really need.

Prayer introduces us to our authentic needs. To know our true need is to become intimate with ourselves. When we become intimate with ourselves, we disclose our divinity both to ourselves and others.

We can join genius, create new intimacy, create new God and when we do that as a community, there is nothing more stunning than that.

That is the new church. That is the new world. That is the new synagogue, a world in which we are a Unique Self in an intimacy, in a Unique Self synergy, in a Unique Self Jazz Symphony where we are playing our unique instruments to address every need of intimacy in the world.

What we are saying here in Evolutionary Church is that **the world is suffering from a global intimacy disorder. It is only the restoration of intimacy that heals the source code, that awakens the new humanity, that evokes the new human, and that unleashes the next stage of evolution.**

Unleashing the next stage of evolution is utterly necessary in order not to be annihilated by existential risk.

Existential risk happens on many vectors, whether it is rogue terrorist bombs, or the rape of the environment, or people going to sleep alone at night desperate for companionship, or people who are going to sleep with a person that they shouldn't be with, which is desperate in its own way, or all the failures of love which cause the explosion of #MeToo. The whole thing is a failure of intimacy. There needs to be a hashtag *#IntimateUniverse*, a hashtag *#OurUniqueIntimacy*, and a hashtag *#WeAreGodsUniqueIntimacy!*

We go into our holy and our broken *Hallelujah*. We can't bypass it, and when we come out of the holy and broken *Hallelujah,* we are going to pray.

We are going to offer up our deepest need and we are going to say, *please, please God, give me this*, because prayer affirms the dignity of our need, the holy and the broken *Hallelujah*.

It all matters.

We invite everyone; I invite myself, every part of me; we invite all of us together to offer a prayer and ask for everything!

To be intimate with myself is to ask for everything, not just for world peace.

Get to world peace, yes, but what do *you* need?

What do *I* need?

Let's offer up our prayers, and let's impress them on the lips of God as we fall into the Infinity of Intimacy. We join together, and we link our hands, and we link our hearts and we create a field of intimacy and we open up all the gates.

Remember our code: *Evolution is the process of ever deepening intimacy.* Evolution is the evolution of intimacy. *Amen.*

EVOLUTION IS LONGING TO GO FROM NO-THING TO EVERY-THING

Let's take the evolution of intimacy on a universal scale. Speaking about the text, *The Universe: A Love Story,* from the beginning, from the Big Bang, let's add ideas from the book *Cosmos & Culture,* by our friend Howard Bloom. He is talking about the desire of the universe itself for intimacy:

Three hundred thousand years after the Big Bang came another mass astonishment, a radical act of sociability: "the big break." The particles in the plasma slowed down and gave each other more space, but these puny particles called electrons, for the first time in their 300,000-year existence, were not satisfied on their own—it's just like us!—They had an electromagnetic hunger, craving for a sort of sociability, and sociality that this universe has never known.

When we say *the interior of us is yearning for intimacy,* we can go down to the quarks and the electrons.

They discovered they had an electromagnetic longing at their core.

Remember we said: *Evolution is longing.* How did it get from no-thing at all to everything—and to evolution as it is now continuing through us?

If you and I had been around to bet on the outcome of protons' and neutrons' new electromagnetic lusts, the last thing we would have guessed is that these social drives—see how important this is—would bring electrons and protons together in tight synergies and they fit perfectly.

See, this is a universal intention of God, and here is one of these words that I am just learning from Howard Bloom:

I call this sort of thing manic mass production and super synchrony—you know about synchronicity, but this is synchrony—it refers to those landmark events in which the same thing happens at the same time all over the face of the Cosmos...

Imagine that for a moment: The universe is designed in a way that synchronic synchrony was at work 13.73 billion years ago. Listen to this:

When roughly ten to the 88 nearly identical quarks precipitated at precisely the same time from the space-time manifold, from a spreading sheet of feed and there were many types of them but only eight to 18 in the Cosmos, that is supposedly "random."

He has put "random" in quotes indicating that this massive organization at the quantum level, which was perfectly designed for quarks to find

110

each other—and with roughly ten to the 87 identical copies of each quark existing in synchrony, this is highly unlikely. This is *manic mass production* of intimacy on a scale that defies belief.

I want to bring up the idea of developing a greater trajectory of intimacy among ourselves. It is awesome to realize that every one of us is made up of the trillions and hundreds and hundreds of quantum billions of entities attracted to each other within us to make us a new whole system. It seems to me that these quarks, these electrons, these protons, these things, this intimate essence of the physical universe that is inherent in us, is totally matching up within us when it gets attracted.

In the past it was attracted to sexuality, to the awesome Reality of being able to have a sperm get an egg and create an organism, and out of that organism are these trillions and trillions of particles who have to turn to make a heart or a lung.

The lovers don't really know what's happening. They have no idea.

Let's see how would we join, at least just two of us for a moment, and then we can go up to more of us. We have used the phrases "whole mates" and "supra-sexuality." What is that in terms of the intimacy of evolution?

Let's take supra-sexuality. Imagine that unique frequency of someone's essence, and imagine it fusing with the essence of somebody else's being that you love, such that the essence of you fuses with the essence of the other.

Let's assume that the same perfection of synchrony that brings the quarks together is bringing us together so that in the intimacy of evolution, of supra-sexual union, the frequencies are doing something new.

You wouldn't necessarily know what it is. Just like the lovers don't know about sperm and egg, the super-sexual partners may not know about the deeper cosmic intimacy.

Let's expand that imagination to the church. Let's say everybody here, we are all electrically charged when we feel connected, with attraction and repulsion always happening. It's okay not to know, but do say *Yes* to being in this. Let's offer this to everybody here together, uniquely, who we are with whatever partners or supra-sexual creative unions we are blessed to have. Let that grow.

Everybody here is attracted to being in the Evolutionary Church. That means the frequencies and the unique essence of each of our beings are apparent enough in order for us to join genius in the church. Wow. Imagine all of us simultaneously in a church, in *this* church, because we have been drawn together by attraction to something that we would say is the impulse of the church itself, which is to bring love into the world—to bring in the Evolutionary Love frequencies such that our society, which is so separated, so devastated, so antagonistic, can thrive. As we join together with each other, let's imagine us bringing it out into the world and not just telling people about it, but having the power to attract them to their own inner frequencies, joining with each other and with us.

It reminds me of the story of the first Pentecost and of what happened to the disciples in the upper room after the death of Jesus. They all began to hear in their own voice what everybody else was saying, and Peter got up and said: *how is this possible? We are all Galileans but these people are speaking other languages, they are the disciples*, and Peter said, *this is what has been prophesied by the prophet Joel: in the last days the Lord will pour Spirit on all flesh.*

The planetary Pentecost. The awakening of humanity. The purpose of this church!

Hold this. Say within yourselves: *what is the state of my heart?* Tune in to the state of your heart as an expression of the universal creativity joining us together.

ATTRACTION, INTIMACY, AND ALLUREMENT

It is not just attraction, it is allurement! When you don't experience allurement in every piece of your life, the only move you have is to always sexualize allurement.

Sex is awesome. Sex is beautiful, and it is a disclosure of Eros, in the right place, at the right time, with the right person, but **we have exiled allurement to sexing.**

When you have exiled allurement to sexing, and you don't feel allurement in every dimension of your life, you are going to cross inappropriate boundaries, and you are going to begin to objectify.

The men will be objectified for power and the women will be objectified for power or body. It is a tragedy! But when I awaken to intimacy and the *inside*, I realize that the inside of attraction is intimacy.

This is so deep; this is so beautiful. It is not my or anyone's personal message, it is *one message*, it is one love. One message, one love. Can you feel that: one message, one love? Feel this for a second! Our colleague Fritjof Capra talks about attraction, but attraction is the *outside*, and the *inside* of attraction is intimacy.

The *inside* of attraction, the *interior* of attraction is intimacy.

The interior of intimacy is allurement.

Attraction is this outside force; it is this physical force of attraction.

It is true, it is an exterior expression of the interior. We talked earlier for example about electromagnetic attraction, which is the interior allurement of Reality expressing itself, manifesting itself outside.

What we're saying together in this Evolutionary Love Code is that process of electromagnetic attraction, that new disclosure 380,000 years after the Big Bang, was a process when electrons realized *we have to dance, we have to dance! We can't do it ourselves.*

What is dance? How does dance work? The Hebrew word for dance is *mechol.*

Do you know what *mechol* means? The dance of electrons and protons.

The dance.

What drives the dance? It is an allurement to each other that allows us to trust our bodies that will be in synchrony with each other, and we will always fall in the right way, and thus we'll be creating the larger whole of a dancing pair, a dancing dyad or triad.

All the quarks at the first moment of the Big Bang were in threes. They were in *ménage à trois*, they were doing threes.

We are not just dyads. We have whole mate dyads, but then we also have triads. Our friend Dave Logan wrote an entire book on tribal leadership which was about the next level of consciousness going to the Holy Trinity, when there are triads.

For example, our team here, we are a particular form of triad. We work together. That does not eliminate dyad between each one of us. The dyad is the dyad. That never disappears. Then we create a triad.

Then we expand even further, and we create a community based on intimate communion. We create a community based on Outrageous Love, when we are not just figuring out how this is serving me: *Am I getting my needs met? I am a consumer, does the church fill my needs?*

Hello? Blank that! No, no: I *am* the church! I am *allured!* We are allured to each other.

When we don't really experience allurement, then we exile allurement to the sexual, and then we ask the sexual to fulfill our entire need to be allured. Then the sexual collapses in a *#MeToo* eruption because it can't bear the weight of our need for allurement.

We want to feel allurement every place!

Just like evolution itself is ever deepening intimacy. Ontogeny and phylogeny recapitulate each other. This means that the history of evolution and my own evolutionary history are *one* history. That's what we're saying:

- One love
- One evolution
- One allurement
- One message

Within that *one,* there is not fusion. There is the uniqueness of each person—it's all there—but **we come together as a new configuration of intimacy, which is evolution's ever deepening intimacy.**

We get to be allured to each other. When one of us is giving their message, I am allured, I am inside, I am listening. I am not preparing my message. The only thing I can do is just be allured by someone's talking. We are allured when someone is writing something. We turn to the writing, and we are allured. I am allured to every single person here.

When **we create a Field of Allurement, that becomes Unique Self Symphony**. In a Unique Self Symphony, the instruments are allured to each other, yet they are independent. They are in this Field of Intimate Communion.

Then **we move forward, and we create a politics of allurement.** A politics of allurement means that if you're hungry, I'm hungry. If you are brutalized, I am brutalized. If 305 people died in a mosque from terrorism, something in me died in that mosque, and I'm inside that mosque, and I feel the explosion, and my heart rips apart in pain.

And, there is gorgeousness all over the world!

Right now! Right now all over the world there is gorgeousness happening! Babies are being born all over the world in this moment. There are explosions of beauty happening, and we feel those. In this Field of Allurement, we wake up.

PSEUDO-ALLUREMENT, PSEUDO-EROS, AND THE NEED TO CLARIFY MY UNIQUE SELF

In this Field of Allurement, I find that my Unique Self is my unique set of allurements.

To clarify my Unique Self is to clarify my allurement.

Pseudo-allurement or pseudo-eros or pseudo-intimacy is when I can't bear the loneliness. I can't bear the emptiness.

I impulsively move to create instant intimacies, project after project, book after book, business after business. It doesn't matter what it is, in order to cover the emptiness, because I can't bear it. I am 14, or I am 27, or I am 15, and I can't bear it. I can't bear it, I can't sit in intimacy with myself, I can't sit in the hole and let the hole fill up with my natural intimacy.

- Pseudo-intimacy destroys worlds.
- Pseudo-eros destroys worlds.
- Addiction is a form of pseudo-eros.
- Instant intimacy is a form of pseudo-eros.

We can recognize each other. We can be intimate and then we have to work, to deepen the relationship.

We must look at the field. We must distinguish, to clarify between my authentic allurement and pseudo allurement.

My authentic allurement emerges when I can sit in the hole, feel the pain of it all, when I can stay in.

116

My authentic allurement emerges when I don't look to fill myself up with a pseudo-allurement, or pseudo-eros, but realize that my own evolution is my own ever deepening intimacy when I stay in the hole.

Here is my absolute promise: Stay in the hole! Stay in, stay in, stay in and then it will fill up with your authentic intimacy.

Here is why we trust each other. There is no one here who doesn't fall in the hole.

> A person that you can trust is a person who can sit in the hole, can feel the clench, can let go of the pride.

The pride cometh before the fall.

A person you can trust can let go of the pseudo-pride. Pseudo-pride is a pseudo-allurement to yourself. **I am going to sit in the hole and then I am going to trust the truth of who I am which is: I am God's unique intimacy.**

I am going to know that and to trust that.

With trusting the intention of Reality in manifesting the unique configuration of intimacy which is me-ness, the hole then fills up. It fills up with genuine allurement and genuine Eros and genuine connection. I am going to tell you something hard, my friends: sometimes you sit in the hole for 15 minutes and sometimes you spend 10 years moving in and out of the hole. If you stay in, it will always fill up with your gorgeousness.

Always, always, never not, oh my God!

What a delight for us to fall in love. What a delight to be with all of us whole mates here. To feel this happening together, to come together and to love it open, to love it open together in this Field of Allurement, in this Field of Intimacy, that is unlike any other.

Your love is lifting me higher than I have ever been lifted before, because that is what allurement does. It raises us up.

117

I want to invite us as our love lifts us higher, and as we chant, to open up the space of grace. We chant to each other and we say: *How could anyone ever tell us*—how could anyone ever tell us in this Field of Allurement—*that we are anything less than beautiful? How could anyone ever tell us that we are less than whole? How could anyone fail to notice that our love is just a miracle and how deeply we are connected in our souls?* That is the field of allurement: how deeply we are connected in our souls!

We are going to evolve, we are going to write the source code together.

I am allured. I am allured. Your love is lifting me higher! I am allured. Let's feel the allurement waking up in us! Oh my God!

Da Vinci danced in Florence as they were bringing in modernity, which raised all boats.

We want to dance our way into enlightenment!

We want to dance our way into awakening the new species!

We want to dance our way into what we call evolving the source code!

We want to dance our way in joy and ecstasy and in urgency, because it needs to happen in order to create tomorrow.

CHAPTER EIGHT

ALLUREMENT, AMAZEMENT, AND EVER INCREASING INTIMACY

Episode 58 — December 2, 2017

EVOLUTIONARY LOVE CODE: EVER INCREASING INTIMACY

> Deepening intimacy, radical amazement, and wonder: the practice of ever increasing intimacy.

> Emergent newness is setting a frequency of attraction.

Let's just begin in our resonance with remembering the Big Bang. There are those who say it is continuing to explode within us. In that Big Bang, in the first flaring forth, the structure of matter and consciousness and life was structurally set down perfectly.

It is so fascinating to see that for 13.8 billion years, the attraction to greater intimacy of separate particles has been happening and thus making a new whole greater than the sum of the parts.

That is nature's plan!

Think first of the quarks. I love the quarks! They are coming together, and they are creating, and then we have the formation of electrons and protons. When you

observe at the quantum field level, you affect what you observe. This is scientifically true.

It is true at that level. We are going to take it all the way on up. Feel now the attraction within you that came from this Big Bang.

Every single cell within you is attracted to make an organ. Can you imagine the organic intimacy of an eye or a heart or hands throughout you, throughout all of us?

Feel your body vibrating in the resonant field. Cell with cell, organ with organ, billions of cells with billions of cells. They say there are 52 trillion cells—in you!

And what are they doing? They are being attracted to each other.

You are a body filled with love. Let's awaken to the intimacy of the particles vibrating in your body. To feel it as a body vibrating with the attraction, particle to particle making a whole, and when we open our eyes, we can see other whole systems, the genius of evolution. Just realize that the self-organizing being that we are is mad up trillions of cells self-organized, and the Self is a big capital S.

That Self is attracting us now to each other.

The global intimacy disorder is a disorder that's been able to work in bodies and in small groups and in cultures for hundreds of thousands of years, which is now being reawakened in you and me.

We are overcoming the global intimacy disorder.

Wherever something emerges in evolution that hasn't quite happened before, it is setting the frequency of attraction for other cells everywhere on Earth who might wish to feel this intimacy.

Put your attention on a unique love for somebody you are attracted to and feel the irresistible power of intimacy in Evolutionary Love.

We can have Evolutionary Love that is totally universal and we can bring it down to the most intimate being that you are attracted to. When you come together with someone that you are intimately attracted with, you are co-creating more who *you* are, who *we* are, and who *we all* are.

My friends, when we get intimate, we whisper to bring us into intimacy. We are saying, *Come closer like this*, as Rumi says. How beautiful is it to start with a whisper?

The Universe is giving us an opportunity to listen carefully.

The entire story that we are so excited about is about this idea, this Evolutionary Love Code:

The strange attractor of evolution is ever increasing intimacy. Deepening intimacy, radical amazement, and wonder, or the practice of ever increasing intimacy.

The strange attractor of evolution is new intimacies and then ever increasing intimacy. Let's just look at it for a second between human beings. Why do we come together? We come together because we are excited about each other. We see each other with fresh eyes.

DEEPENING INTIMACY AND THE BIRTH OF EVOLUTIONARY CHURCH

When Barbara and I met, we were in completely different realms. We had heard of each other vaguely, you know, kind of moving through the world, but basically doing different things in different times. We had one good mutual friend. But then at one point we got together because a friend of ours got us together for a dialogue, and as we did the dialogue, we felt an allurement.

Oh! Oh! Allurement!

I have talked to thousands of people. Barbara has talked to thousands of people. We both love talking to people.

But there was something else here. There was a unique frequency allurement that said, oh, let's create intimacy, let's come together, and let's see if we can join genius. Something wants to be born here. Of course, it did not happen in a second, but it started to happen.

Then the challenge to that is you get used to it. You get used to it. You kind of take it for granted. You are allured originally, you fall in love, but then you don't go to ever increasing intimacy.

Barbara and I learned to practice, **how do we do ever increasing intimacy**? How do we spend time in Holy of Holies joining genius and convergence?

We have to *practice* ever increasing intimacy, so our quarks can go *quark, quark, quark, quark*.

That is what quarks do. Everybody knows that. *Quark, quark.*

We *practice*, and we say to each other always, *come closer like this*—and here is the big word—**we let ourselves be radically amazed.**

RADICAL AMAZEMENT AND WONDER: THE PRACTICE OF EVER INCREASING INTIMACY

Whenever I talk to Barbara, we want to hold each other in radical amazement. We want to be in wonder, and I will tell you a little secret, okay? There are interior sciences! We want to be validated by exterior sciences and interior sciences. *It is not just exterior sciences*, Mr. Sam Harris. It is not just about the way the brain works in neuroscience.

We want to hold together this deep sense that the way the brain works—and this is exterior science—is that when you have a conversation with someone, your brain decides what you are going to say before you know.

Your brain gives you a quick read, a scan of all the situations you have ever been in, and it says, *this is how you should respond.* You never choose. You are always on automatic pilot, even with someone you love.

How do you break that?

Intimacy is about originality. Intimacy means it is an original moment. It is the original face before your mother and father were born. It is fresh. It is audacious, erotic, sensual, and new.

In German, there is a word, *Frechheit*. *Frechheit* means it is new, it is audacious.

- How do you hold the newness?
- How do you hold the audacity?
- How do you not get into a pattern?
- How do you not forget to appreciate?

Every time Barbara does something so stunning, and then I forget because I just expect that stunningness. And then I am asleep, there is no more ever increasing intimacy. If I ever take for granted the letter that I get from Barbara in the morning, then I am dead! I can't take that for granted! That is the most gorgeous thing in the day.

What do I need to do? How do I create ever increasing intimacy?

Radical amazement and wonder. We know in brain science that what breaks rote repetition is radical amazement and wonder. That is the brain science. **When you are surprised, amazed, full of wonder, then the rote of the brain is broken. Then you are kind of broken open again. You are loved open. And then all of a sudden, you are original.** Isn't that wild?

The way the brain, in neuroscience, does an original thought is by becoming intimate once again.

How did Madonna say it in that sacred text? *Like a virgin, touched for the very first time*, meaning **you make love with the moment, like for the very first time. That is what an Evolutionary Lover does.**

That is ever increasing intimacy. Because this code that Barbara and I formulated together, and we are formulating all the Evolutionary Love Codes together, and we invite everyone to add into them, to comment on them, to make them better. Let's make them ours. These are *our* codes!

What we said was not just that evolution is the evolution of intimacy, which is one code, but we said, **the strange attractor of evolution is ever increasing intimacy.**

ROTE REPETITION STANDS AGAINST EVER INCREASING INTIMACY

What stands against ever increasing intimacy?

- Rote repetition.
- Failure of gratitude.
- Failure of radical amazement.

What breaks rote and repetition, what allows for intimacy, which is the original virgin moment? It is what allows you to *get newer* every day.

How do you get newer every day?

You are intimate with Reality every day.

Every day.

Gorgeous! Wow. I mean, wow!

I am getting so excited now! It is so exciting I get to be here with my beloved whole mates and with every single person in this church. I am just radically amazed at this delight! And Barbara whispers to us and says, *come closer like this!*

And friends, rote repetition can be even our pain, even our holy and broken *Hallelujah.* We can get used to being in pain. **We can get used to our suffering. Even that becomes not original.** I will tell you something wild: **You have to make even your pain original.** Even your sadness, you have to make original.

You have to get intimate with your sadness. Then it starts to dissipate. It starts to melt from the delight of the intimacy because it is fresh.

Even depression, you have to refresh. When you refresh your depression, it disappears.

We get in a rote. We get in a rote of being sad. We get in a rote of broken hearts.

In prayer, I bring my holy and broken *Hallelujah.* I bring the outrageous pain that I feel in life, and the outrageous beauty that I feel in life. I bring the Outrageous Love, and I offer my holy and broken *Hallelujah.* Let's now turn to Leonard Cohen, "Hallelujah."

We offer ourselves, and we say, Oh my God, *quark, quark!*

We ask for everything. Ask for everything. *God, please!*

God is the Infinity of Intimacy that knows our name. Prayer affirms the dignity of personal need. And we ask for everything afresh, anew.

Quark, quark.

ATTRACTION OF INTIMACY IS GOD'S PURPOSE

I am overjoyed to realize that this attraction of intimacy that we feel for each other is God's purpose. I want to speak for a moment of the awesome nature of evolutionary purpose that uses intimacy to ultimately express God's purpose.

Evolution creates newness by joining particles together by attraction. The quarks have no idea what they are getting started with, but when they get attracted, nature makes new particles out of those quarks. Then nature creates this gorgeous single cell that is the most awesome thing, and it lives for a couple of billion years.

Then suddenly it is not working. It is running out of energy. And, what does nature do?

Attraction!

Even though they don't like each other, they get attracted, and they create multicellular organisms by attraction, which then brings down this power of solar energy, and the whole planet bursts into life.

We can take this process up and down the entire evolutionary spiral.

> *What is God's purpose? Our attraction is not simply helped by God's purpose. It is God's purpose.*

To see God's purpose—which, as I've mentioned many times before, I gained from my favorite Catholic Jesuit paleontologist, Teilhard de Chardin—you look at the whole spiral. Nature, God, is creating greater consciousness with every joining of every one of those particles, single cells, multi-cells, animals, humans, and *us* on planet Earth.

The global disorder is *yearning* to come together. That is God's purpose, his consciousness.

But God's purpose is also for freedom. So, as we come together and join genius and love one another, we don't just lose our identity.

We become *freer*.

That is an awesome quality of the way love and consciousness works. There is no doubt whatsoever that *Homo sapiens sapiens* becoming *Homo universalis* is becoming ever, ever freer than the early humans, or the animal humans, or the first animals, and so forth.

Look at our freedom! God put the power to destroy an entire world in those thermonuclear bombs. And we are free to create them. Think of this as we're free to explore our ever expanding consciousness—**this brings the human race into this awesome dilemma.**

Then let's name the next things that happen:

- ◆ We have consciousness expanding.
- ◆ We have freedom to create and to destroy, which God put in there; it is not an automatic universe, it is not run by God in that sense.
- ◆ Then what he put in there was love.

Here is how God put love in: **In order to become more, to become newer, to become fully your potential self, you have to join separate particles to make a new whole whose consciousness increases through—we might call it—synergistic love.**

You are how many trillion cells?

They have to love each other! They have to get together, to be attracted, and out of that comes the awesome individual.

Now, in this time, we individuals on planet Earth with our global disorder are being attracted to each other. And **wherever we are being attracted to** each other with this type of power, you can be sure that the God force of creation is making us newer, is making us more intelligent.

For example, I can have a desire of wanting to be a global speaker, as I really do. I have that view for myself, but when I ask, *why I'd want to be a global speaker*, I'm realizing my attraction to a Planetary Awakening in Love through a Unique Self Symphony. And my attraction within this is process is: *I'd like to be a voice to speak to everybody in the world who would like to know the next stage of evolution.*

Why? **Because it's my gift!**

On the other hand, it couldn't make the slightest possible difference unless everybody else, who is giving their gift, was joined by their incredible, synergistic, loving, organizational capabilities to create the awesome reality of radical newness.

Right where we are now, in this exact moment of history, is the shift point on planet Earth. This phenomenon of attracting together to create newness is carrying us over one side of the tipping point, and this separation, and competition, and destruction of each other is carrying us to the other side of the jump.

> *God does not care for species.*
> *God cares for purpose. We are in*
> *the sixth mass extinction, but the*
> *difference is that we know it.*

Therefore, at the shift point, it is absolutely fascinating that we are all internally shifting.

We are the fortunate generation to live at the precise shift point of planetary devolution or planetary evolution, and every one of us is at

the tip of the tipping point of evolution—connected through our joint intention.

Let's contemplate for a moment the awesome Reality of the genius of the process of evolution, however you want to see it: God, Source, Spirit, internal order, etc.

Of course, we want to be scientifically accurate, but it is also true that **there's no capacity in scientific accuracy to describe the purpose and impulse of evolution.**

They can't do it.

In fact, they deny it often. They say, it is just a random, beautiful, magnificent, accidental universe.

Excuse my language, but that's stupid. I want to acknowledge that everybody's impulse a Planetary Awakening in Love through a Unique Self Symphony is also God's purpose—radically and powerfully.

We will find, if we know this, that we are intended to put our full passion into it no matter how painful or sad. **The purpose can guide us through the planetary shift together, not alone.**

I thank God for this.

Thank you, everyone.

Let's contribute to the planetary awakening in love. It is like with the early Christians who believed in the Second Coming of Christ. This belief in the second coming of humanity, this belief in humanity doing this, is what we are contributing to. To do this, we are going to have to be as great as we are. We are not contributing to an outside cause. We are contributing to our own unique gorgeousness to be part of this, and guess what, it is happening in our lifetime.

Amen. Amen. Amen.

We are at the moment of either evolution or devolution. **We are either going to rise! We are either going to let our love evolve and lift us higher, or it is going to fragment, and it is going to disappear.** The existential crisis that faces us, the existential threats to our very existence, are exponentially unlike any of the sets of threats that any generation ever experienced.

We are at what Rilke calls *the pivoting point.*

We know that which can lift it up is an evolution of the source code, is the Evolutionary Love Codes.

This is the moment.

This is the time.

We are the ones we have been waiting for, and it is up to us to do this. We believe, and we're sure that more than any other structure, this *dharma* is critical.

Awakening the new species is critical. This is the moment when we can be in the convergence zone, where we entering into the source code itself.

There are those of us who are allured. It's allurement. Intimacy is a quality of allurement. I want to be intimate with you because I am allured to you.

THE EXTERIOR AND INTERIOR OF INTERCONNECTIVITY

Here is the story. High tech gives us *interconnectivity.* The new powers of high tech, which are key to the quality of what some call (beautifully) *Homo universalis*, those new qualities of high tech are essential. And *Homo universalis*, this new species is made up of what we call Evolutionary Unique Selves.

Interconnectivity is the exterior quality of the new high technology. It's an interconnected world. There is a quality of interconnectedness in the exterior sciences, but then **the inside of interconnectivity is intimacy. The inside of intimacy is allurement.**

Wow! I am allured to give my gift, and my gift can be given by no one else other than me, and a Unique Self Symphony—because what we are all about here is a planetary awakening in love through Unique Self Symphony—is our entire commitment. That is everything we dream about. We want to shout it from the rooftops, but since the rooftops need exponentializing, we want the rooftops to be a billion people rising. The vision is not as a fanciful dream, not as a kind of wild, strange imagination, but as a true imagining. We are *Adam. Adam* in Hebrew means *the imagining one.*

---

*We are not just Homo sapiens.
We are Homo imaginus.*

Let's imagine it. Imagine it, but as a reality, because you can only imagine that which already exists. You can't imagine something that doesn't exist. Let's imagine this together! Let's imagine it together: Here we go, there are ten million people in Evolutionary Church, and there are Evolutionary Churches all over the world. And everyone here is a minister of their own Evolutionary Church. There are ten million people in Evolutionary Churches all over the world, and those ten million people are a central node. **Imagine!**

There are Evolutionary Church ministers and Evolutionary Love ministers all over the world, and we are a ministry of Evolutionary Love. We are becoming the new human. We are evolving the source code. Imagine it now. Let's bring it down. This is the power of intention validated by all the interior sciences. And the exterior sciences will catch up.

Amen! Hallelujah!

We are *intending* this now, and **our intention is powerful, and all obstacles are melted away.**

Are we excited? We are excited!

Are we evangelicals? Of course we are!

We are bringing the good news. We are preaching it together. We are *being* it together. Let's imagine it! Ten million people! I am crying! Ten million people. Do you understand? Do I understand? Do we understand? That would change the world! It would be a different world. Those ten million people are the central node, the leading edge of the leading edge. We are allured to each other, and friends, **here's the key: sometimes we contract, and sometimes we clench because we're imperfect and we all make mistakes. But we always unclench, and we always, fearlessly, own our responsibility—and we *always* reestablish intimacy anew.**

Every day!

It is not that we don't fall. It is not that we don't contract. It is not that we don't get upset with each other.

Of course, we do! It is not that we don't lose allurement. We lose allurement—and then we re-allure. We reignite. And our love lifts us higher.

Allurement that lasts forever and never changes, just unceasing allurement all the time, is pathological. That is not the nature of allurement. Allurement emerges and then it recedes.

There is a hard day, and then you write a beautiful letter, and you are re-allured. And I write back, or I write another four paragraphs, and the Goddess comes in, and She writes for me. I say, *oh my God, I feel it again,* **but I never lose the trust that it is there.**

I am always re-alluring.

THREE STAGES OF ALLUREMENT IN MYSTICISM

In mysticism, stage one of allurement is called submission.

It is kind of like falling in love. You are blown away. Oh my God, he is my teacher! She is my partner! He is my friend! I am allured! I want to join. I want to be part of, I am submission. I am fully submitting. I am filled with praise. I am delighted. I am in love. For example, in one expression of allurement, your partner says, *hey, do you want to see a movie, honey?* And you say, *sure.* Your partner says, *well, what movie would you like to see?* And you say, *honey, as long as we are together, it doesn't matter at all.* You know that stage. You are in. *Do you want to move to Alaska, honey? Sure. Let's move tomorrow. Not a problem.*

You get it, right? Like we are in. We know the truth of allurement.

And then, even in the most noble and beautiful people, something happens. All of a sudden, *ahhhh, I can't find it anymore!*

I am going to tell you a little secret. A lot of times the reason we can't find it anymore is because of life, life in its pain and in its *sound and fury.* The threats of life. Physical threats, emotional threats, existential threats, intrude on us. We contract, clench, protect, and we are afraid—and sometimes we should be.

Life is hard. Life is not easy. We get attacked. Maybe we get attacked internally. Maybe we just can't hold it steadily. We don't have object constancy. We all have traumas from someplace or somewhere.

Level two of allurement is separation.

I don't quite feel the allurement, but I stay in. You get it? I stay in. I look for it again. I look for it again. I do the work, and I say, *you know what? I am making mistakes, but I know I am making mistakes in the right direction. And I am going to do the work of allurement. I am going to stay here and do it.* Then, what always happens is an absolute promise of Reality because allurement is true: I re-allure. I reawaken. I get to level three.

Level three of allurement is called radical *sweetness*.

It is the steady allurement where I have regained level one, but now at an entirely new level of consciousness. Sweetness! Do you see that? That's level-three allurement.

You might think you get to level three and you are home. Nope, it doesn't work that way. You keep cycling through all three levels. That is the nature of Reality. In one day, in one conversation, you can go through all three. But what you know is you know the truth. Your center of gravity is level three.

You know how you know that?

Because you know that allurement doesn't live alone in your skin-encapsulated ego. That allurement is going *quark, quark, quark*, right?

It is the nature of Reality itself. Awake, alive, becoming conscious in you. And then what you begin to do is, and here it is, ready?

ALLUREMENT IS A CHOICE

These are the big two words: *Choose allurement!*

I choose to be allured. I *choose* the truth of allurement.

When I choose the truth of allurement, I begin to wake up. I begin to become powerful. And I begin to become potent, and possibility opens.

When I choose allurement, the possibility of possibility emerges.

I choose allurement.

We are writing the source code. We are rewriting, we are evolving it together.

I choose allurement.

I choose allurement.

Once I get that, I know that I have to correct one word.

First, *I* choose allurement. Then, *we* choose allurement.

We go from I to we. We choose allurement as a Unique Self Symphony.

I choose allurement. We choose allurement. You can feel Goddess.

You can feel Her delighting. You can feel Her dancing. She is dancing in us. She is dancing as us. She is present.

If you want to know what Goddess is saying right now, I give you my absolute word.

Goddess is saying right now, three words: *We choose allurement*.

That is what She's saying, we choose allurement. My love is lifting me higher, higher than I have ever been lifted before. My love is lifting me higher than I have ever lifted before when we choose allurement because that is who we are. We *are* allurement. It is the essence of who we are.

In this moment, in this convergent zone, as we are ready to go from devolution to evolution, we close with a concluding blessing: I choose allurement with everybody so that we form a Field of Allurement in the story of evolution at the tipping point. We are having an effect throughout the world where anybody is tending toward allurement.

That is the way nature works.

Our shared allurement is affecting all the people who yearn for allurement worldwide.

Allured and new every time.

Thank you, God.

CHAPTER NINE

A NEW ORDER AND THE
BLESSING OF THE FATHER

Episode 59 — December 9, 2017

OUTRAGEOUS LOVE IS THE INTIMATE NATURE OF REALITY ITSELF

There is so much bad news out there, and that's hard. I think we all have that experience. As we open up the news, we don't get a sense of the gorgeousness of Reality that is happening in every second.

- We don't get a sense of the mother holding the baby.
- We don't get a sense of the tenderness between beloveds.
- We don't get a sense of the intimacy that is holding Reality together in so many ways.

All of that **gorgeousness of Reality that is happening in every second**, from the very first nanoseconds of the Big Bang, from the very first quarks that go *quark, quark*, to this very second, right now, where there are billions of human beings tenderly loving, talking, communicating, holding, and being with each other in such exquisitely, dignified, beautiful, and gorgeous ways. When we open the vehicles of our communication—the press, the news, the nervous system of our planet—we don't feel that beauty.

The news focuses on the mistake, the pathology, the aberrant, the tragedy. All of that does need to be reported, but it needs to be reported in the larger context of truth.

I, Marc, spoke to a very dear friend of mine. We were chatting, early in the morning. I said to this person, *how are you feeling?* And this person said, *well, so-so.* Then we looked at it together and laughed! We said:

> *Well, how's your kidney doing?—Awesome!*
>
> *How are your livers?—Fantastic!*
>
> *How is the circulatory system?—Oh my God, so good!*
>
> *How's the million miles of nerve cable?—Unbelievable!*
>
> *How are the 100 trillion cells?—Fantastic!*

We went through the context of so much allurement, so much intimacy, so much good.

But instead, we do—and all of us do that—what we call the *missing tile syndrome*. The missing tile syndrome is when you find the *one thing* that is wrong. It is when I am completely focused on, *Oh my god, where am I going to be for New Year's? Oh my god, my book, my book is not in with the publisher, I am so behind, I am so devastated by that.*

We find the *one thing* that is painful to us. We put all of our energy into that one thing, and then we lose our Eros. We just get deflated.

I am going to tell you something secret. I am not amped up, I am just *in* Reality. It is not being amped-up—this is the *nature* of Reality. The nature of Reality is, *Oh my God, my kidneys are working.* **I am feeling the goodness of Reality moving through me.** That is the truth. I feel the Intimate Universe holding me every second.

Not that I am unaware of the missing tile. Believe me, I am aware of the missing tile! I know a little bit about outrageous pain. That is why we say:

The only response to outrageous pain is Outrageous Love.

We don't mean to cover up the outrageous pain with some amped-up, New Age, supercilious, naive ignorance. That is not what we mean. We mean Outrageous Love. **Outrageous Love which is the very intimate nature of Reality itself.**

In mysticism, we say, **Outrageous Love is love before creation,** because it is not reactive. It emerges from the depth in the nature of Reality itself. That is why Outrageous Love, or what we call Evolutionary Love here, is the good news.

If we are anything, we are the ministry of Evolutionary Love. We feel Evolutionary Love in our coming together and our joining together. We feel each other's pain, but we also feel each other's joy. We feel delight in each other.

This real deep understanding of intimacy will take us into the code.

EVOLUTIONARY LOVE CODE: THE EVOLUTION OF INTIMACY

The evolution of Reality is the evolution of intimacy.

The new level of evolutionary intimacy is Unique Self Symphony.

We come together not just as individuals, not just as Unique Selves, not just as Evolutionary Unique Selves, forming the great *Homo universalis. Homo universalis* is made up of what I call Evolutionary Unique Selves.

We feel the joy of growing and *symphonizing* together. We wake up to this in the morning. We are thinking about this all the time. We think about this in the middle of the night. We wake up at 4 a.m. thinking about it. We think about it at 4 in the afternoon.

The urgency of the evolutionary impulse keeps us up day and night.

INTIMACY IS SHARED IDENTITY

What does it mean to go to the next level of consciousness, to respond to the existential crisis, by creating a new order of humanity, and by becoming a new human, and by awakening a new species?

By what?

By invoking, inviting, a planetary awakening in love through Unique Self Jazz Symphony. That is what our code is about. What does it mean to be part of a Unique Self Jazz Symphony? **The essence of the whole thing is intimacy.**

What does *joining genius* mean? It means to be intimate. It's no longer just an "I"; it's a "We." In a "We" there's no fusion because the "I" doesn't get lost. The "I" is a rock star. We're not joining genius by going into fusion. The "I" does not get lost in fusion.

I want to give you a definition of intimacy: **Intimacy is shared identity.** Is that crazy? Shared identity. Not fusion, but *union!* Shared identity.

I am going to tell you something so dramatic and so beautiful that it is just going to blow your heart away. *Shared identity*—it took me 20 years to say that simple sentence:

Intimacy is shared identity.

Once you say it, it is obvious. Well, I am slow, it took me 20 years to articulate that meme.

I am going to give you another crazy thing. It is so crazy!

The entire Christ story is about shared identity.

Jesus said, *I love you so much—I could cry when I say it. I love you so much. I want to be so intimate with you that I am willing to share my identity with you.*

You know what that means?

That is what we mean when we say *the word became flesh (apotheosis).* In other words, God says:

> *I love you so much, I am infinitely perfect, I am the best speaker and orator and writer in the world, but I don't care. I am going to share my identity with you. I am going to join genius with you. Your pain is my pain. Your joy is my joy. That is the Unique Self Symphony. I want to join your world in Unique Self Symphony, and we are going to share identity. I am no longer a solo act. I am playing my instrument gorgeously, but I am listening to you. We are symphonizing together. We are sharing identity.*

We are a Unique Self Symphony, and we are sharing identity. We are enacting, activating, the Unique Self Symphony. We are bringing it down.

PRAYER IS SHARED INTIMACY WITH GOD

As we go into our hymn, we listen to Leonard Cohen's holy and broken *Hallelujah*. We offer our holy and broken *Hallelujah* because God says, *if your Hallelujah is holy and broken, then my Hallelujah is holy and broken.* God says, *bekol tzaratam lo tzar, I am with you intimately.* God says, *I love you so much, I am willing to share my identity with you.* Oh my God! We turn to God and we say, *we are going to offer up on Your altar our holy and our broken Hallelujahs,* and then we pray. We are going to **ask for everything**. We are going to **pray for everything**. We are going to know **we delight the Divine in articulating our need**. We are inviting God to love us open and give us everything.

We step into the holy and the broken *Hallelujah*.

We turn to the Divine and say, *We love You so madly that we want to be You. We want to share our identity with You.*

My friends, do not be a spectator like the Greeks were! Step in and love it open with your prayer! With your personal need, ask for everything.

Feel it.

Prayer affirms the dignity of personal need.

I invite you with such gentleness, such tenderness—*pray*! When you write your prayer down, something happens. The neuroscience of writing, the interior science of writing, is that when I am willing to make that effort in my hand and write a prayer, something opens up. It is the depth of it happening in me that opens up the depth happening above, because **we are shared intimacy with God.**

When I open up, when I speak it, when I write it, something happens, something moves. We turn to the Divine and we pray, and when we pray, we ask for *everything.*

Unique prayer is a component of that fulfillment. The glory of the fulfillment of life's purpose *together* is the Unique Self awakening in love.

FULFILLING THE STORY OF CHRIST THROUGH A PLANETARY AWAKENING IN LOVE

I am reminded of St. Paul on the road to Damascus. He was out there attacking the Jews, as you know. At some point, he had a complete, total experience of the resurrected Christ, who came to him and said, *Why are you putting all of these pricks into me? Why are you doing this?* St. Paul was completely blinded by the glory of what he saw. He came back and the person persecuting the Jews became new, because he'd had a vision of the resurrected Christ.

The calling for a Unique Self Symphony is a *vision*. Maybe we have seen glimpses of it, and maybe it has something to do with the resurrected Christ, that is to say, **a being who would go beyond the limitations of the current situation into a new being, a new life, a new world**.

I tend to admire St. Paul deeply. He started to write letters. Those letters ended up forming little churches. At first, they were forming just little circles of people who were able to draw on the image of the resurrected Christ, which fulfilled the story that he was crucified and spent the three days in the tomb. But Jesus did come out as himself, but as a new being. He didn't come out just as a cosmic mystery. He came out so he was recognized by Mary. This story is *exactly* right. While we are fulfilling our spiritual, social, and scientific, technological capabilities, **we are *exactly* fulfilling the story of Christ**.

Let us go back and see what happened in those early days, and see what is happening now, that could be related to that. In the early days, Jesus said something very strange before he died. He said, *Take, eat, this is my body. Take, drink, this is my blood given for you.*

The most intimate expression!

I used to know some Catholic sisters, and I spoke to the sisters of St. Joseph. They called me a Catholic because I have this huge sense of expectancy. **That sense of expectancy is expectancy for the planetary awakening in love!**

This is the same thing as the resurrection and the eventual *Second Coming of Christ*.

In all these small circles, they did communion. I remember because I was with the Catholic sisters quite frequently. It had to be a priest, only he could do communion. He was all dressed up, and they all went up, one by one by one, and they would drink the wine and eat the wafer blessed as the Body of Christ. The entire Catholic Church is eating the Body of Christ, oh my God!

I thought, well, why don't we do that ourselves? That was sacrilegious from a Catholic point of view. But I got a signal from God: *Take communion every day.* So, I got a little knapsack and put in a bottle of wine and crackers. I would visit friends and I would say, *would you like to do communion?* Nobody wanted to, but I got them to do it anyway because I had the wafer, the wine, the crackers, and the desire.

So, we sat down, and we did it. We said, *I take this body of the living God that I am consuming inside myself, to become like that, by giving my voice in the Unique Self Symphony, toward a planetary awakening in love.*

That is comparable to what Jesus called for—*the Christification of the Earth,* as Teilhard de Chardin said it. We're not using religious language because it's been narrowed, but we are using the power of this story.

Let us imagine together a Unique Self Symphony that includes everybody's voice.

Do you remember St. Paul on the road to Damascus? All of us are on the road to a planetary awakening in love—*this is the real thing!*

EROS BIRTHS ETHICS

A new order is a new configuration of intimacy. We have been talking about this deeply—what are the next steps?

It will take time, and we are looking at huge next steps.

- We're talking about what it would mean to unpack a vision of evolutionary ministers
- What would it mean to unpack a vision of a new order?

We're taking it a step at a time. It's wild how the impulse moves together in these early visions. It's a Unique Self Symphony—that's exactly what it is.

144

The Eros of a Unique Self Symphony yields the ethics of a new Unique Self Symphony.

We are going to look at the last scene of the movie *Dirty Dancing*. It is not known as a sacred text. It is an unconscious sacred text of public culture about Unique Self Symphony.

In the last scene of *Dirty Dancing*, it's been a complicated summer. Johnny, that is Patrick Swayze, and then Jennifer Bray, her name is Francis, her nickname is Baby. It is summertime at Kellerman's resort in the Catskills. When you are at a resort in the Catskills—I have spent many years in that world—you are in your own world. There is betrayal. There is love. There is loneliness. There is heartbreak. There are false accusations—all the complexities of life.

And now, as a result of the entire story of the summer, the God and Goddess, that is to say Johnny and Francis, are separated. The scene opens, Francis loves Johnny, Johnny loves Francis, but the circumstances of life are keeping them apart. She is sitting at the table with her mother and father. It is the last moment of the summer. It is the closing dance.

You can notice, as the scene opens, there is no Eros. There is no Eros and there is no ethics. (Eros always births ethics. Eros is always about the ethical.)

They are sitting at the table, but it is supercilious, it is surface, it is not deep. People are milling around. There is no symphony. Everyone is busy and having surface chatter, a little gossip. Nothing is really moving in the room. We see the dance on the stage. If you noticed what they said about the dance in the beginning is that it is "lovely". Yawn! Nothing is happening.

And then he decides, Johnny says: You know what? I am going to show up. I am going to wake up. I am going to grow up. I am going to get over being right. He walks in and he walks over to her table. She is sitting with her father, who completely disapproves of him, and she wants the Blessing of the Father—and don't we all want the Blessing of the Father? Her father completely disapproves of him, but he walks over and he calls her to him. She says, *you know, I have to step beyond the father.* She walks over to him and they walk together on stage and they interrupt the music.

At this Kellerman's there are two kinds of dancing. There is public dancing, which is very polite and very lovely. It is 1963! Then there is dirty dancing. But here's the thing even the movie is unconscious of: *It is not dirty dancing!*

There is nothing dirty about it. They couldn't find the word for it. You get it? They didn't get it. They didn't know. Even the filmmakers didn't. The scene has it. They didn't have the language for it. They didn't know how to talk about Eros. So they call it *dirty dancing.*

That is the most pure scene in the world, nothing dirty about it in the world. But by dirty dancing they mean: It is deep Eros. The quarks are coming alive in that.

What happens? What does he say? How does he open the scene? He says: *I introduce my dance partner Francis.* Who is she? She's a person who stands for truth and integrity, for what is right, *no matter what it costs.* That is Eros! **Eros births ethics. And ethics births Eros.**

Then he says, *She calls forth and demands that the best of me shows up.*

By *the best,* he doesn't mean the best dance moves.

He means the most loving, the most ethical, the most intimate.

That is true Eros.

> *It's not about sex, and it's not about doing it right! It's about Eros. It's about the actual life force of Reality coursing through you, awake, alive and moving, and you know that it's ultimately significant.*

The reviewers of the movie thought it was about a nice romance. This is not about a romance in the Catskills! Are you for real? Did you all miss the entire point? This is an incarnation of God and Goddess. **When Johnny and Francis are on that stage, they are Evolutionary Unique Selves. They feel the entire energy of evolution coursing through them as they dance.**

When we dance, we trust our bodies; we trust our hearts. We know we are going to fall.

As they begin to dance and they begin to move, something moves in us. He walks down, he jumps off the stage after dancing with her, and he invokes the Unique Self Symphony. People begin to dance. All class distinctions fall away. All economic distinctions fall away. The African American waiter, in 1963, begins to dance with the patron. In all of Kellerman's—this Catskill resort, that is built on the split between the staff and the upper middle-class guests—it all falls away, and all of a sudden the place explodes in dance.

There you have Unique Self Jazz Symphony happening right in front of you.

It is Eros.

It is Eros that births ethics.

Do you get it?

There is Eros that births ethics. There is love in that room.

Old distinctions fall away, the coiled contraction of the ego unfolds and people are gathered in a new order of being, in a new way of becoming.

We cannot invoke the new human, we cannot awaken the new species, without Eros.

Eros which is:

* We are allured to each other.
* We are attracted to each other.
* We are willing to stand for what is right, no matter what the cost.
* We are willing to stand in radical integrity.

They just blow my heart open. What she has to do is to be willing to give up the Blessing of the Father, to leave that table and go with Johnny. Then when her father in that scene at the end meets her and Johnny, he says, *Wow, I was wrong.* Then he looks at his daughter and says, *Oh my God, you were beautiful up there!*

He is not being a leering dad talking about her sexually. God forbid. He is saying, *you were radiant, you were beautiful, you were wiser than I was!*

THE BLESSING OF THE FATHER IN UNIQUE SELF SYMPHONY

We are invoking all of our dads here in all of their complexity. Can we invoke the Blessing of the Father and give each other the Blessing of the Father? That scene was an expression of Unique Self Symphony.

What is our vision?

That is our vision! That is our vision, right there! That scene was it! That is the vision. That is Unique Self Symphony. That is the *energy* of it. That is what it *feels* like. That is the *delight* of it. That is the *Eros* of it. In the last scene, you saw Unique Self Symphony happening. Let's just take a look at this.

The shadow is the frenzy, the frenzy of dance with which we get lost. But this scene here is not the frenzy of dance, it is not frenzy. This is symphony! It is love. It is respect. It is integrity. The invitation is to create together a new order.

We're going to talk about how to do it in so many ways. We just want to look each other in the eyes, and we want to bless each other, and we want to give each other the Blessing of the Father.

Can we be fathers to each other?

Can we say to each other: *your dance changes the entire room?* It is not frenzy, but it is beauty.

Can we say:

I give you the Blessing of the Father.

We all want and we all need the Blessing of the Father. I just want to invite us to that place, where we give each other the Blessing of the Father.

I give you the Blessing of the Father. The father that so many of us did not have, or who was not what we wanted him to be, or the father we weren't able to be ourselves.

Can we give each other the Blessing of the Father?

> *I give you the Blessing of the Father...*
> *I give you the Blessing of the Father!*
> *Father, come closer!*

What gets in the way of Eros is we think we don't have the Blessing of the Father. So, we are afraid. But when we have the Blessing of the Father, he can look at us and say, *You are radiant! You are beautiful!*

When I don't have the Blessing of the Father, then my Eros gets distorted.

Then I have to cover up the emptiness. The loneliness is too intense. We have to find each other and give each other, in Unique Self Symphony, the Blessing of the Father. We are fathers to each other. We need to say it to each other: *I give you the Blessing of the Father.* It is such a big deal!

So much blessing to *my* father who passed away. He will allow me to say this: I always wanted a different father. It didn't work for me. It was painful for me. He was never the person I wanted him to be. What do I do with that? I wanted him to be great and I thought he was petty. I wanted him to be expansive and thought he was contracted, and now I am thankful. I thank my father for *everything*. And I give him *the blessings of the son*. And I ask you to give *me* the blessings of the father. And I give *you* the blessings of the father.

That is what a Unique Self Symphony does. The reason Jesus was so powerful is because **Jesus had the blessing of the Father to be Christ.**

Christ says: *I am erotic. I share my intimacy with you. I share my identity with you, and I give it freely all the way.*

Deepest blessings to all of you.

Amen.

CHAPTER TEN

TIKKUN: YOUR UNIQUE FIXING IN THE EVOLUTIONARY PROCESS

Episode 60 — December 16, 2017

EVOLUTIONARY LOVE CODE: YOUR UNIQUE FIXING

To be intimate with Reality is to know your unique *tikkun*, your unique fixing, the unique reason you are here.

That the universe in some profound sense needs only you and specifically you to do this specific act. That when you do it, it's your expression of divine evolutionary impulse that is most needed to fix or heal or evolve something in the universe.

Getting in touch here with that intimate Reality of your unique fixing.

Breathing into it. Realizing that the design of evolution is perfect.

For all the failures and distress and pain in the world.

The fact that you exist with that unique fixing for some aspect of it, and so does everybody else, reveals a pattern of meaning in the universe itself.

Let's resonate with that unique expression of healing, of fixing. Feel it fitting into exactly where it belongs, where it fits best to heal exactly what you want it to heal.

See if you can remember the first experience of that impulse and its divine purpose in this world, and allow it now to fix that which **only you can do and are now doing, in this exact moment of attention to it, and your intention to express it, the whole way**.

We want to bring an image, which is one of the most utterly beautiful images ever expressed by the light masters, by the great revolutionaries, in the history of planet Earth. It's a founding image of evolutionary spirituality. The masters of evolutionary spirituality, Schelling and Fichte, wrote about it in Germany, having enormous influence on us, on Sri Aurobindo, and on Teilhard de Chardin. The image is also in response to someone who said, *Why talk about brokenness in church?*

It's an image from the Hebrew wisdom tradition about what happened before the first moments of manifestation. Before the first nanoseconds brought, what we also call in Kashmir Shaivism, *the 32nd Takla,* the moment of manifestation.

Before **manifestation is not before the human being; it's before the great flaring forth**.

- What was there before there was anything?
- Where did it all come from?
- What's the initiating impulse of everything?

There's a description by Isaac Luria, who had enormous influence—there are tens of pages of scholarly influence, scholarly notes, on Luria's influence on Fichte and Schelling. Isaac Luria is called the Lion of Shafat—the *Ullah Khalil,* the Lion of Shafat—who lived in northern Israel in the late 16th century.

In this image, he goes into one of the greatest mystical revelatory states in the history of humanity, and **he sees a phallic penetrating light which**

enters into the vast emptiness, the vast empty space. Then ten vessels of light come to receive and to hold the space. The light is so intense, so powerful, that the intensification of the light shatters the vessels.

Shards of vessels, broken pieces of vessels, *Shevirat haKeilim*, are spread throughout Reality.

Then evolution begins, and ultimately evolution is going through its stages, from quarks to atoms to molecules to cellular to multi-cellular, all the way up to human beings, and then, ultimately, to conscious human beings.

> *The entire purpose, the entire direction, the entire delight of evolution, is to become conscious—to awaken.*

When evolution awakens then the human being—the conscious human being—begins to be the liberator of light.

The human being finds the broken vessels, and the broken vessels are the broken hearts, the broken dynamics, the broken economies, the broken relationships.

We live in a world of utter perfection, and we live in a world of broken hearts and broken vessels. We live in a world of outrageous pain.

But the human being awakening as conscious evolution, as the liberator of the light, gathers the sparks of light and liberates the sparks of light from the darkness of the vessels.

Every human being has one vessel—one broken vessel—that is theirs. That spark of light, which is needed to move evolution to its next stage, can only be liberated by that person.

There's nothing that I can do, ever, no matter what I do, or how hard I try, to liberate the spark of light that is yours to liberate.

I can't do it.

But there is a broken vessel that waits and cries and says, *liberate me, free me, heal me.*

The Force, as it were, awakens in me (because *Star Wars* just came out last night with their new movie).

- The Force is the force of liberation.
- It is Outrageous Love.
- It's the outrageous stuff that's not *reactionary.*
- It's not ordinary love, it's Outrageous Love, which is the heart of existence itself.
- It's Outrageous Love which is the initiating and animating Eros of All-That-Is.
- It's the Force that lives in you, as you, and through you, that has a unique perspective and a unique quality of intimacy, that can actually stand up to the abyss of darkness and liberate a spark from a broken vessel in a way that no one that ever was, is, or will be can.

We call that, in our code, *our unique fixing.* Sometimes we use the Hebrew word that's entered into language, the language of evolution, which is your unique *tikkun,* your unique fixing.

Do you understand the delight in knowing that? *Oh my god, there's a unique fixing that awaits me.*

A great student of this tradition was none other than Leonard Cohen. Leonard Cohen directly studied this tradition, and when he talks about a *holy and a broken Hallelujah,* he's directly—not abstractly, not metaphorically—he is specifically and directly (as he said in an interview towards the end of his life) talking about a musical prayer that captures precisely the code of this week: that every human being is born to offer up their holy and broken *Hallelujah*.

My broken *Hallelujah* is like that broken vessel, that broken heart, that broken dynamic, that lives in my unique circle of intimacy and influence, that's mine to fix, and no one that ever was, is or will be, can fix it other than me.

All of Reality needs my fixing.

May the Force be with us—the force of fixing, the force of *tikkun,* that lives outside and lives in between all the rocks and the stones, and lives in everything. Nothing is devoid of the Force, and it lives in us. May the Force awaken in us, the Force of fixing in me. And that's our prayer for today: may we identify that broken vessel, that broken heart.

Paradoxically that doesn't put us in pain, that lifts us from pain. It brings us into a radical joy, the potency and passion of purpose and delight, and knowing we are utterly needed:

- I fix with my laughter.
- I fix with my tears.
- I fix by embracing the fullness of my dignity, my joy, my wonder, by coming before God.

And saying:

- God, master of the universe, who lives in me, because I'm also a master of the universe.
- I'm going to co-create with you.
- I'm going to do this with you,
- I'm going to liberate that spark.

LIBERATING THE BROKEN VESSELS

Let's allow ourselves to tune into God, the original source and purpose of universal evolution. Because if all have a purpose to fix something, let's go back to the original God force.

Occasionally I put my attention on what it would feel like to be God. If I am the Creator, what is my deepest impulse?

It's to create co-creators.

We are created in the image of God, and that original impulse in the first two seconds, as I understand it, was so perfectly designed, that **if the energy and matter had been slightly different it could not have formed energy, or matter, or universe, or hydrogen, or anything.**

This perfection at the origin of creation, in that flaring forth, God's purpose—let's assume it to be as perfect as the scientists are unwillingly discovering it to be, because they don't believe in it. This perfection that is all the way up the chain of life. The fixing is exactly how you are meant to evolve.

Fixing the broken part is also fixing the open part that is calling you to your uniqueness.

I want to just tell you an amazing thing that has been happening. This is a huge scale fixing that we are called to.

In my (Barbara's) brother-in-law Dan Ellsberg's book *The Doomsday Machine: Confessions of a Nuclear War Planner*, the question was whether we should drop the first atomic bomb in order to defeat the Nazis and possibly Japan? To fix a terrible thing with an even more terrible thing?

156

You can see the dilemma of the fixing here. Is it right to fix, using an atomic bomb, the destruction caused by Nazism and Japan if it should attack us? This is what these scientists were seeing. It wasn't just the atomic bomb, it was going to be the nuclear bomb. Then it could be the thermonuclear bomb.

Dan was a consultant at RAND Corporation and was studying this. What he noticed was that the people who wanted to fix the problems of these other societies that were destructive were, as he writes, *proposing as a solution the annihilation of humanity*—and these were the most intelligent people that we could possibly find to be fixing our problems.

Obviously, the Russians were also going to be fixing. Because they had to fix us for wanting to fix them. There was actually no Missile Gap.[11] They were way behind us. But John F. Kennedy went roaring forward on these "fixings."

The Missile Gap, which didn't exist, led the Russians to build up their nuclear arsenal in order to be able to threaten us with nuclear annihilation.

This is continuing now, the vast number of thermonuclear weapons we have to "fix" each other.

The first thing to notice here is the complete and total irrationality at the highest level of intelligence, of scientific military intelligence, in these cultures, and now in other cultures as well.

What would we actually need to be fixing with the fixing of the fixers? They were trying to fix it in such a way that it was *an annihilation*. The thing about thermonuclear weapons is that—and this is the phrase they used— it's a *decapitation of a culture*. It burns it up alive.

---

11   The Missile Gap was, in essence, a growing perception in the West, especially in the USA, that the Soviet Union was quickly developing an intercontinental range ballistic missile (ICBM) capability earlier, in greater numbers, and with far more capability than that of the United States.

General Curtis LeMay was the man who proposed this with a vicious attraction to doing it. And they thought it was all good.

Take a huge breath here. Take a huge breath of the evolutionary impulse of creation going back to God the Creator who created such potential for intelligence, that he created the opportunity for co-creators to destroy the creation.

That is the ultimate freedom that God put in the system.

The ultimate potentiality of the evolutionary perspective, the evolutionary potential, is actually to take that power that is residing in the atomic energy, the whole nuclear power, the whole high-tech power, and evolve it to the stage of co-creation in the world.

Let's look at this as an epic moment in the history of evolution, in the history of God's purpose, of *tikkun,* and let's put ourselves personally, you and I, in that story of fixing that which is broken. But the brokenness is being developed by those who think they're fixing it, those who are more or less in power almost everywhere. The boldness of us fixing those structures that have, in a certain insanity, developed the power to destroy everything in the name of security.

We need to see what this actually means in the nature of this moment of evolution, from the perspective of God having created intelligent creatures capable of understanding creation—and, through science and technology, able to create that which they feel can help fix Reality.

WE ARE A UNIQUE SELF SYMPHONY FIXING THE SOURCE CODE

A Unique Self Symphony is emerging. Let's bring that into the fixing because perhaps it's the only way big enough to fix the fixers, as well as that which is genuinely broken.

The Unique Self Symphony would be those of us who have something to fix, to create, joining together in a symphony of energy:

- The vision of this Unique Self Symphony would be that everybody on Earth who has an impulse of love, creativity, uniqueness, of fixing something, would be doing it in the same period of time.
- Is it possible that the awesome destructiveness of those who are supposedly making us secure and empowered, whether it be in the old form of capitalism or in the military-industrial complex—that this is the call for the most awesome power of the Evolutionary Lovers of the world?
- That the Evolutionary Lovers had to meet up with something this awesomely dangerous, in order for us to be called forth with abandon to give our gift to that which only you can fix.
- Let's imagine the same God that was able to create the Big Bang with absolute perfection of the energy and matter at that moment is also doing it now.
- What would that mean if we are as good as the Big Bang? I remember Andrew Cohen used to say: The Big Bang has never stopped, it's happening every minute.

Let's end with imagining each of us being called:

- To fix the fixings that are potentially destroying the world—*annihilation* is the word.
- To evolutionary potentiality through a Unique Self Symphony which comes into a planetary awakening in love.

Let's imagine now: there are millions of fixers fixing the fixers, and we are going to conclude this thought with the glory, the joy, of being a fixer.

Each of us is fixing something.

I keep thinking that if I'm fixing more knowledge of conscious evolution, I'm helping to fix everything. We have to laugh at that too, but it's true.

Let's fix that unique thing we are called to do, each one of us, somewhere in this broken world. Or you might say in this evolving world, evolving through these crises.

Let us imagine that what we are intending is the nature of the Big Bang. It is why it all got started in the first place.

If there is any reason at all for the Universe, it is to contribute to its fixing.

I feel that the fixing of the fixers is going to be initiated as part of the exact purpose of evolution.

And it is just such a delight to be here, *whole mating*, or joining genius.

We don't join genes, we join *genius*. It is when teachers can shatter even the notion of their being individual and apart, to create shared space. All the mystical traditions say when the hidden egos of teachers are shattered, and they come together to love each other: *the Messiah will come.*

PSEUDO-FIXING AND AUTHENTIC FIXING OF THE SOURCE CODE

We pointed out that fixing can destroy. Daniel Ellsberg, who we have sat and talked to, is a wonderful man. His unique fixing, his unique *tikkun*, was to get involved in stealing appropriately, breaking the law, stealing documents, and leaking them in the public space, which became the Pentagon Papers. (Thank God that Barbara's dad was not in prison but was there to help with the legal bills or it would have been a big mess.) Daniel Ellsberg did this great unique fixing. This audacious act.

What a story!

Now what is the question always going to be? What's my unique fixing?
Here's how we get there. This is so deep because we're going to fix the source code.

I received an email from Andrew Cohen this morning. He's a wonderful man who's gone through his own crisis and shattering and rebirth and reteaching. Whenever someone goes through a crisis and says it, as Andrew has, that *I've really looked into my life and I've apologized and I'm transforming and I'm going the next step*, we always invite them to go the next step. So, we're loving and honoring Andrew.

Andrew and I (Marc) had a fierce argument. You can go online and search for a book called *Self in Integral Evolutionary Mysticism: Two Models and Why They Matter*. That book was based on my argument with Andrew. It was about what we said earlier. I want everyone to get this:

---

*The most important thing we can
do is to fix the source code.*

There's a reason that the *dharma* matters—not the *dogma*, but the *dharma*. Fixing the source code and knowing the distinctions matters. The reason is that when the distinctions are sloppy, New Age sloppy, then actually the philosophy that emerges destroys the world.

The original and most public form of evolutionary spirituality that dominated the world was communism. Communism came directly out of Hegel. It was directly out of this notion of evolution that Hegel wrote that absolute spirit was moving forward, and that we were going to fix Reality.

Whenever there are people who are trying to fix Reality, when they don't have an accurate source code, beware.

- Robespierre's *reign of terror* in the French Revolution.
  They were trying to fix.

161

- Communism's killing of 17 million collective farmers. They were trying to fix.
- The United States' taking on the Soviet Union in the Cold War in ways that were insidious. They were trying to fix.

That is what we are pointing to. This is why we are changing the source code—it's why we're doing this—because the source code itself hasn't been evolved. After my (Marc's) big argument with Andrew Cohen (and Andrew is wonderful, by the way), he wrote to me about a year ago and told me, *Wow, I got it.* He came on board. And, I've been happy in other conversations where Andrew has shown me important things, but in this one, Andrew says, *I get it.*

Let me tell you what the argument was about. This is everything, I'm going to tell you a story. The argument was about a phrase that Andrew had called *Authentic Self.*

This is really important. We are doing a fixing here.

Andrew's phrase of Authentic Self meant the evolutionary impulse awakening in you. Andrew was beautifully impacted by Barbara's important work. He was a Neo-Advaita guy, then at some point he said, *No, no, I get evolution.*

He did a big transformation and he started talking about evolution!

Andrew started talking about the Authentic Self. He called the Authentic Self that which is beyond your True Self, your classical enlightened self. He said there's an impersonal awakening in you of the creative evolutionary impulse. You move beyond the personal, and the impersonal evolutionary impulse awakens in you—*you* leave.

In his book on evolutionary enlightenment, he talks about the personal all through the book, about 80 times, as something you have to move beyond: *The personal separate self, the personal is personality. You have to get to what Advaita Vedanta calls pure True Self, and then you awaken beyond it, impersonally as part of the process. The process always dominates the personal, and the personal always interferes with the process. To awaken as enlightenment, you become the process.*

That is exactly half right. **When it's only half right, it is so wrong.** The destruction that can come from it is beyond imagination.

Andrew and I did five fierce public *dharma* combats on this. The first one was in front of a thousand people in Tel Aviv. They were always done with integrity, as we fought not personally, but with integrity. This is why we're doing what we're doing, why we're fixing the source code.

How do I know we're right? Because it's a genuine direct realization—a thousand percent clear. Not everything is equally right. Some things are more right than others. Andrew was partially right. There *is* something beyond True Self. **There *is* beyond just becoming part of the One. There *is* a creative impersonal impulse that moves in you.**

- ◆ Level one: separate self—personal.
- ◆ Level two: I'm not a separate self; I am part of the all. I am essence, I am True Self.
- ◆ Level three is actually not Authentic Self, which is impersonal. *It is Unique Self*—the personal comes back online.

It is after you have clarified that you are no longer part of separate self, you are True Self, which is the One, or the process. **In Advaita Vedanta terms, the True Self is the One. In evolutionary terms, the True Self is the *process*,** meaning you are beyond separation—I'm part of the process, the process has awakened in me. The evolutionary impulse is awakened in me. That's step two.

But then, when you awaken even more deeply—when you enlighten more deeply—you realize that beyond True Self is Unique Self.

Unique Self is when the personal comes back online. It's not the broken grasping person; it's the Infinity of Intimacy that lives in you and me. It's the personal face of the evolutionary impulse, which is your Unique Self and your Evolutionary Unique Self.

Why does that matter? It's everything.

Every person is irreducibly unique and gorgeous, and the dignity of every human being comes from the personal quality of intimacy they incarnate.

You can't destroy half the world in a nuclear strike. It's only when you have the early broken idea of evolutionary spirituality—which is beyond the personal (separate self) and is just the impersonal, and you have to become part of the process that you have to fix the process by killing a few million people.

If it's only about the process, then that's what you do. Lenin said: *You have to break a few eggs to make an omelet.*

No, in our omelet everything is needed for the recipe. We are a Unique Self Symphony and every instrument matters. We are born as a *Tinok,* meaning baby in Hebrew, and every *Tinok* has their unique *tikkun,* their unique fixing.

That's why distinctions matter.

The reason distinctions matter is because to not get this is a disaster. In other words, we distinguish between what we're going to call *pseudo-fixing,* or fake fixing, and *authentic fixing.*

Authentic fixing is, I fix from the place of my irreducibly unique gorgeousness, which is irreducible—I'm not a cog in a machine. It's not just impersonal. After the impersonal is the personal at a higher level: the Infinity of Intimacy that lives in me, and my irreducible dignity.

I am willing to stop the saving of the whole world to help one person.

You get it? Anyone who saves one life has saved an entire world. Anyone who heals one tear has changed the entire world.

That's why when we have told the story about Yoselle in Krakow, who would leave the little notes under the door, we realized it's so important to say that what he was doing was part of the evolutionary process.

STORY OF THE MASTER ISAAC OF BERDITCHEV

Here's a story that captures our beautiful message to distinguish between the broken fixings or the need to fix the fixers, and authentic fixing. The difference is we must first fix the source code.

That's why at Evolutionary Church and the Foundation for conscious evolution and the Center of Integral Wisdom, our first commitment is to fix the source code, because that fixes everything.

It is a most beautiful story. It's a favorite story of Barbara and I that we've told each other back and forth, from Easter a couple of years ago, when we were in the tomb of Metamorphose together. A beautiful story, and it's about *Yom Kippur*.

Yom Kippur, which is a holiday, the holiest day of the year. *Yom Kippur,* mystically, is the evolutionary holiday. It's the day when all worlds are mystically fixed. The activists in Hebrew mysticism thought they could actually change history by going into the internal, highest heavens and fix the whole thing.

> There was one master, Levi Isaac of Berditchev. He is on this fast, and they're fasting for 24 hours. He's the prayer leader. He, with his voice, is rising. He's finding his way. It's like an Ayahuasca journey, not that I would know anything about that, but he's way in.

> And he's finding his way to the highest place.

Yom Kippur is a 24-hour fast, and it's now close to the time when it's about to end. You know how that is, everybody is starving. But they've forgotten that they're starving because there's so much ecstasy. Because he's now the master in the highest place, in the highest heavens, and he's finding his way in.

And he's about to bring the *Messiah*. Meaning that all of evolution is about to explode in perfection. All good is about to be accomplished.

And then as he's about to fix it all, he sees out of the corner of his eye, an old man who's 94 years old, who's thirsty, and he needs a glass of water because he's so uncomfortable. After all, he's fasted for 24 hours. He desperately needs a glass of water.

The great evolutionary master, Levi Isaac of Berditchev, stops everything, and he comes down from the highest heavens, and he ends the fast and drinks a glass of water. He goes and he gets a glass of water, and he brings it to that man, and he says: "This is the fixing that has to be done right now."

When I (Marc) heard that story, I cried for an hour. I heard it when I was maybe 16, when I was reading the back of an Aramaic text at the end of a book. An Aramaic text. The story was recorded. The story is so important because it fixes the fixing. Does everyone get that?

We're in the holidays when suicide rates spike, and people are alone, and people are desperate.

Reach out to someone and fix it for that person. Or call someone who no one's calling.

No one is extra. No one is left out. No one is outside of the circle.

And if the fixing requires wiping out half of humanity, well it is not a good fixing. But it's more than that. If the fixing involves leaving anybody outside the circle, then it's not a true fixing. In a true fixing, everyone's fixed.

I wrote Werner Erhard the other week and asked him what his contribution is to this new framework that we're trying to articulate in the Foundation for conscious evolution, the Center of Integral Wisdom, and in our Evolutionary Church. Werner said, *My contribution is to create a world that works for everyone.*

Just an email a couple of weeks ago. A world that works for everyone.

A true fixing is a world that works for everyone.

To do that, I have to go first—I have to heal my own fixing. I have to know that:

- I'm a broken heart.
- I'm a broken vessel.
- I have to be fearless in fixing my own fixing.
- When I fix my own fixing, then I can fix the world.
- I am a fixer.

We want to write that into the source code—to really know: *I am a fixer.*

I invite everyone to find that identity: *I am a fixer*, and we write it into the source code of Reality.

Let's say it together if you can: *let's build a world that works for everyone.*

ABOUT THE AUTHORS

Dr. Marc Gafni is a visionary world philosopher and futurist, one of the leading formulators of world spirituality and religion of our time, and a beloved teacher and public intellectual. He holds his doctorate in philosophy from Oxford University, as well as Orthodox rabbinic ordination. He co-founded the activist think tank, now called the Center for World Philosophy and Religion, where he serves as the co-president with Dr. Zachary Stein. He also served with Barbara Marx Hubbard as co-president of the Foundation for Conscious Evolution, which he consented to lead at Barbara's request after her passing.

He is known for his "source code teachings"—including Unique Self theory and the Five Selves, the Amorous Cosmos, a Politics of Evolutionary Love, a Return to Eros, and Digital Intimacy—and has more than twenty books to his name, including the award-winning *Your Unique Self*, *A Return to Eros*, and three volumes of *Radical Kabbalah*.

He teaches on the cutting edge of philosophy in the West, helping to evolve a new *dharma* or meta-theory of Integral meaning that is helping to re-shape key pivoting points in global consciousness and culture, with the aim of participating in the articulation of what Dr. Gafni and Dr. Stein, along with other colleagues, are calling CosmoErotic Humanism.

At the core of CosmoErotic Humanism is what Dr. Gafni and Dr. Stein are calling First Principles and First Values, Anthro-Ontology, and a Universal Grammar of Value. This is the ground of a new shared Universe Story and a new narrative of identity for the new human and the new humanity. This is what they are calling the emergence from *Homo sapiens* to *Homo amor*.

This shared story rooted in First Principles and First Values can then serve as the matrix for a global ethos for a global civilization.

Together with Dr. Stein and Ken Wilber, Gafni is writing a series of seminal books under the collective pseudonym of David J. Temple, which intend to evolve the source code of consciousness and culture in response to the meta-crisis. The first of those books is *First Principles and First Values: Forty-Two Propositions on CosmoErotic Humanism, the Meta-Crisis, and the World to Come.*

Barbara Marx Hubbard (born Barbara Marx; December 22, 1929–April 10, 2019) was an American futurist, author, and public speaker. She is credited with the Wheel of Co-Creation and together with Dr. Gafni, the Wheel of Co-Creation 2.0, as well as the concepts of the Synergy Engine and the "birthing" of humanity.

As co-founder and president of the Foundation for Conscious Evolution and the chair, for the last five years of her life, of the Center for World Philosophy and Religion, she posited that humanity was on the threshold of a quantum leap if newly emergent scientific, social, and spiritual capacities were integrated to address global crises.

She was the author of seven books on social and planetary evolution. In conjunction with the Shift Network, she co-produced the worldwide "Birth 2012" multimedia event. She was also the subject of a biography by author Neale Donald Walsch, *The Mother of Invention: The Legacy of Barbara Marx Hubbard.* Deepak Chopra called her "the voice for conscious evolution."

In 1984, she was symbolically nominated for the vice presidency of the United States. She also co-chaired a number of Soviet-American Citizen Summits, introducing a new concept called SYNCON, to foster synergistic convergence with opposing groups. In addition, she co-founded the World Future Society and the Association for Global New Thought.

INDEX

P

paganism, 21

paradox, 3, 102

particles, 110, 111, 119, 120, 126, 127

pathology, 12, 71, 83, 85, 138

pathos, 87

Pentecost, 113

phenomenology, 128

phylogeny, 115

planetary birth, 7, 8

pleasure, 2

postmodern, 37, 47, 48, 49, 50, 82, 92

power, 8, 9, 10, 20, 38, 69, 70, 71, 72, 73, 74, 75, 76, 77, 79, 80, 81, 82, 83, 84, 85, 86, 87, 88, 89, 92, 95, 96, 97, 98, 100, 101, 102, 103, 104, 112, 113, 120, 126, 127, 128, 131, 144, 158, 159

prayer, 3, 5, 6, 7, 15, 21, 23, 24, 37, 57, 59, 71, 72, 73, 74, 92, 104, 107, 108, 109, 125, 141, 142, 154, 155, 165

premodern, 21, 48, 49, 50, 79, 80, 92

pride, 117

promise, 117, 133

prophet, 32, 113

pseudo-eros, 102, 116, 117

purpose, 3, 9, 10, 41, 76, 77, 78, 86, 99, 113, 126, 127, 128, 129, 142, 152, 153, 155, 156, 158, 160

Q

quantum, 20, 41, 98, 99, 111, 120

R

radical, 41, 99, 100, 110, 119, 121, 122, 123, 124, 128, 129, 134, 148, 155

Reality, 3, 5, 10, 11, 12, 17, 20, 23, 24, 25, 31, 32, 34, 35, 37, 38, 43, 45, 46, 48, 55, 57, 59, 64, 65, 67, 71, 83, 85, 86, 92, 93, 100, 102, 103, 106, 107, 111, 114, 117, 124, 129, 133, 134, 137, 138, 139, 146, 151, 153, 155, 158, 161, 167

realization, 1, 4, 5, 7, 8, 10, 15, 24, 25, 29, 41, 42, 44, 45, 47, 48, 53, 65, 66, 70, 71, 72, 75, 76, 77, 78, 91, 93, 94, 102, 105, 111, 113, 114, 117, 120, 126, 128, 163, 165

reclaiming, 46

relationship, 43, 49, 76, 77, 97, 117, 153

religion, 5, 8, 46

religiosus, 50

remembering, 39, 119

Renaissance, 3, 36, 37, 45, 55, 79, 80, 82

re-patterning, 92, 93

repulsion, 112

resonance, 2, 19, 21, 28, 53, 54, 70, 90, 93, 97, 105, 119, 120, 152

resurrection, 8, 87, 88, 142, 143

revealed, 56, 105, 151

revelation, 75

Rumi, 37, 57, 92, 93, 108, 121

Volume 6 — We Are God's Unique Intimacy

LIST OF EPISODES

www.ingramcontent.com/pod-product-compliance
Lightning Source LLC
LaVergne TN
LVHW011153080426
835508LV00007B/384